THINKING STRATEGIES
for Student Achievement

Denise Nessel
Joyce Graham Baltas

RATNER MEDIA AND TECHNOLOGY CENTER
JEWISH EDUCATION CENTER OF CLEVELAND

Arlington Heights, Illinois
and
Center for National Urban Alliance, Teachers College,
Columbia University, New York

Thinking Strategies for Student Achievement

Published by SkyLight Professional Development
2626 S. Clearbook Dr., Arlington Heights, IL 60005-5310
800-348-4474 or 847-290-6600
Fax 847-290-6609
info@skylightedu.com
http://www.skylightedu.com

Senior Vice President, Product Development: Robin Fogarty
Director, Product Development: Ela Aktay
Senior Acquisitions Editor: Jean Ward
Project Coordinator: Barb Lightner
Editor: Peggy Kulling
Book Designer: Bruce Leckie
Cover and Illustration Designer: David Stockman
Proofreader: Jill Oldham
Indexer: Schroeder Indexing
Production Supervisor: Bob Crump

© 2000 by SkyLight Training and Publishing Inc. and Center for National Urban Alliance,
Teachers College, Columbia University, New York
All rights reserved.
Printed in the United States of America

ISBN 1-57517-265-8
LCCCN 97-76404

2607V
Item number 1924

Z Y X W V U T S R Q P O N M L K J I H G F E D C B
07 06 05 04 03 02 01 00   15 14 13 12 11 10 9 8 7 6 5 4 3 2

CONTENTS

Foreword v

Preface vii

Introduction ix

Thinking Strategies

1 Analogies 2
2 Anticipation Guide 6
3 Cubing 10
4 Frame Paragraphs 14
5 Freewriting 17
6 Graphic Organizers 20
7 I-Search Reports 24
8 Imitation Writing 28
9 Journals 32
10 Key Words 38
11 KWL 42
12 List-Group-Label 46
13 Notetaking 50
14 Possible Sentences 54
15 Read-Talk-Write 58

16 Readers' Theater 62
17 Restating/Paraphrasing 66
18 Saturation Reporting 69
19 Storytelling 73
20 Strip Story 77
21 Team Webbing 82
22 Think-Pair-Share 85

Appendix 89
   Teaching for Intelligence: Parameters for Change 90
Bibliography 96
Index 99

FOREWORD

This book builds on the work of the National Urban Alliance for Effective Education (NUA). The NUA was founded in 1989 with a vision and mission of school reform based upon three beliefs: that all students are capable of attaining high educational standards and that students should graduate from high school prepared to enter a college or university of their choice; that intelligence is modifiable, not fixed; and that all stakeholders in the community must be involved in improving learning and teaching and must commit to address the social, cultural and intellectual needs of students and youth.

The authors of this book, Denise Nessel and Joyce Graham Baltas, are senior consultants for the NUA and in writing this publication strive to provide instructional strategies that support teachers who desire to meet the needs of a diverse group of students. They also provide broad educational principles that can transfer to a variety of classroom circumstances. The ideas they have synthesized build on the work of persons such as John Dewey. Dewey believed that higher-level thinking by students could be nurtured and developed if teachers paid sufficient attention to a student's accumulated experience and sought to develop curricula that would connect with and extend the student experience to real-world application. Dewey has also suggested to his readers that school should be less about the preparation for life and more about life itself (Dewey 1963).

Learning to capitalize on diversity and helping students use diversity as a social and personal resource are also goals of the NUA. It is the hope of the authors that the strategies described herein will also be used to allow teachers an opportunity to bridge between and among cultures in the context of the classroom. Progressive education in the truest sense (at least in our interpretation of persons such as Dewey), recognizes the impact of culture on achievement and contextual learning and, most important, recognizes that instruction should never become a polemic to be used in support of one approach versus another. The rich tapestry of experience that children of color bring to the classroom is something to celebrate, learn from, and extend to children and adults through the fabric of social interaction.

The ideas that Drs. Nessel and Baltas have provided are easily organized by the teacher to support the use of authentic problems and projects frequently encountered both inside and outside of the classroom. The theoretical basis for the work emerges out of the theories of Reuven Feuerstein (1977 and 1978) and Lev Vygotsky (1978), among others, who believe that intelligence is modifiable and susceptible to teaching. Used properly by the teacher, the strategies and lessons in this publication can lead to the in-class leveling of concepts that students of diverse backgrounds and learning can handle and process for deep understanding.

There is a growing body of literature that suggests that when students are provided access to meaning-centered classroom activities that are taught in the context of subject-matter and real-world application, they outperform students who are taught skills that are isolated and scripted. Yet the purpose of this publication is not to advocate for one approach versus the other; what the authors intend is for the strategies that are based on cognitive research in learning to be applied in ways that support whatever approaches the teacher uses that work for their students. They are meant as guides, not as formula. Helping students process text for meaning, and helping students bridge the gap between what they know and do not know are the purposes intended by the authors.

The National Urban Alliance commends the authors for their contribution to the field and looks forward to supporting the dissemination of the publication.

Eric J. Cooper
Executive Director
Center for National Urban Alliance
Teachers College, Columbia University
New York City

PREFACE

What is it that brings about change in instructional focus in the classroom? What are the things that truly allow learning to occur and students to succeed? How can teachers become more effective? What can teachers use to help low-achieving students? These, and many other questions, are ones that we hear daily in our work as consultants with the National Urban Alliance for Effective Education (NUA). This book came about as a result of the work in which we continue to be involved.

NUA members are dedicated to helping all students think and learn. To this end, NUA teachers, administrators, and consultants—in classrooms, workshops, and retreats around the country—share the teaching strategies and learning activities they've found most effective. This is the essence of NUA: the meaningful exchange of principles and practices. We do not offer a program to be followed; we offer an ongoing dialogue about teaching and learning with professional growth as well as student achievement the major goals.

An essential element of this dialogue is reflection—the kind of thinking and discussing that all first-rate professionals do about their work. We're willing to question what we're doing, confer with one another, and change or refine our classroom strategies as needed to improve our work. We're interested not only in how to use various strategies but also in the principles of learning on which they're based, the findings of research that support their use, and the first-hand experiences with them that inform our judgments. Regardless of our relative years of experience or our level of expertise, we seek new understandings and insights about our work with students, and we believe we all have something to contribute as well as much to learn.

For education to be effective overall, the school environment should be safe and secure; students and teachers should be comfortable physically; suitable materials and supplies should be available; parents and other community members should be supportive and, whenever possible, closely involved. All these things are very important, but the emphasis at NUA is on the core of learning: the interaction between teacher and students that—even in the absence of comfortable surroundings, appealing materials, and other externals—makes the most substantive difference in a student's success and satisfaction as a learner. We do what we can to improve the external situation, but our top priority is the way we treat the students as learners—the variety of strategies we use, the kinds of questions we ask to motivate them to seek knowledge, the kinds of activities we arrange to encourage them to use advanced thinking, and the quality of the decisions we make on a daily basis creates and maintains a healthy climate for learning.

Effective classroom interactions keep both students and teachers interested and actively involved. Whether discussing a work of literature, solving problems in mathematics, investigating phenomena in a science lesson, or exploring other cultures, eras, or art forms, effective education starts with teachers and students who are becoming fully literate, who are engaged in critical and creative thinking, and who are on their way to becoming lifelong learners.

There is no single "best" kind of interaction between students and teachers. Just as students have different learning styles, teachers have different teaching styles. The mission of NUA is to recognize and respect the differences among students and teachers while also helping each one broaden and deepen his or her own repertoire of behaviors and skills. This book grew out of this mission and is meant to be a resource that will provide useful suggestions and encourage additional sharing of ideas among its readers.

Use these strategies often. We know that changes in learning will only take place with consistent use of these strategies over time. Finally, enjoy yourself and congratulate yourself because you are taking the time to make learning more meaningful for your students!

INTRODUCTION

The strategies in this book come from a variety of sources. Some are relatively new and have been described by their originators elsewhere in greater detail. Others are related to the excellent thinking practices of earlier generations of teachers and appear here as re-inventions or revisions of those earlier strategies. All are used regularly by NUA consultants in their work in the schools of member districts. As a collection, the strategies give teachers the tools they need to help students navigate the territory of thinking.

THE TERRITORY OF THINKING

The territory of thinking includes modes of thinking, purposes for thinking, and specific thinking skills that can be employed. We'll elaborate on these briefly to suggest the kinds of thought that are incorporated in the strategies in this book.

Modes of Thinking
Modes of thinking are ways of thinking, the kinds of mind-sets that we employ for different purposes. Critical thinking is one example of a mode of thought. When we think critically, we examine something closely in order to make judgments about it. For instance, we listen carefully to an argument and identify the weak links in the speaker's train of reasoning, or we read a text with an eye to identifying the author's underlying assumptions, or we look at a painting to critique the artist's composition or use of color. Creative thinking is another mode of thought. When we think creatively, we want to generate a variety of ideas, come up with a novel point of view, or "think out of the box." What mode of thinking we use depends on our purpose.

Purposes for Thinking

We have many different purposes for thinking. For instance, we might need to think carefully in order to solve problems, make decisions, play challenging games, plan an endeavor, or figure out the best way to implement a plan. Each purpose may include one or more modes of thinking. For example, solving a problem requires identifying or defining the problem, generating possible solutions, selecting one to try, and then noting if it worked or if another solution needs to be tried. At each stage, we might have to shift our mode of thinking to be most effective. That is, we might think creatively to generate a number of possible solutions (being more concerned with quantity than quality at first) and then think critically about each solution to select the best one to try first. As we employ different modes of thought for different purposes, we will also use a variety of specific thinking skills.

Thinking Skills

The specific skills of thinking include such processes as observing, analyzing, comparing and contrasting, synthesizing, constructing meaning, and seeing relationships (to name only a few). These skills can be named as specific entities, but they are most often used in close coordination with one another. For instance, in order to compare and contrast two objects, one must observe them carefully in order to note where they are similar, where different. Such skills are invariably developed and refined in the context of accomplishing some specific purpose. To elaborate further, following are a few ways in which some specific skills might be used for different purposes while employing different modes of thought:

Observing

Consider looking at clouds. You might look creatively to discern animals or faces or shapes. Or you might look critically to determine what weather patterns are forming, given what you know about the relationship between cloud shapes and weather phenomena.

Comparing and contrasting

Consider comparing two different pieces of music, such as an 18th-century sonata and a contemporary rock song. You might make a critical comparison that would focus on the technical elements of the works (the tempo, the instrumentation, the use of refrains, etc.). Or you could make a creative comparison that would focus on the feelings the music evokes, the mental pictures that form in your mind as you listen, or the story that the music would accompany effectively.

Detecting relationships
Consider detecting the causes and effects of a historical event. You might systematically research the major causes of the event and then list the effects that resulted from each cause. Inherent in this process is critically evaluating the source material you're using in doing the research. In contrast, you might put yourself in the position of one of the key players in the event and speculate as to what that person's motivations might have been.

Constructing meaning
Consider working with analogies. The key to understanding and "solving" an incomplete analogy is to determine the nature of the relationship, which requires critical thinking. Once you understand what an analogy is, you can generate an unlimited variety of analogies, which requires creative as well as critical thinking.

Evaluating
Consider making predictions. In order to make a logical prediction about the end of a story, you have to consider the evidence provided by the author, which requires critical thinking. Once you've finished the story, you might then generate a variety of new predictions about what might happen to those characters if the story were to continue, which requires creative as well as critical thinking.

These are by no means all the specific thinking skills that you might want to have students use, but they are examples of what we mean by navigating the territory of thinking. In the strategies that are described in this book, we focus on the types of thinking that are developed and refined in the process of using the strategies.

TOWARD AUTHENTIC DISCOURSE

A concentrated focus on thinking results in classroom discourse that is rich and authentic. By "authentic" we mean dialogue, discussion, reading, and writing that are based on real-world purposes, concerns, and endeavors. The opposite of "authentic discourse" is having to generate the correct answers to a series of questions. For example, instead of asking students, "What color dress was Sarah wearing when the wagon tipped over?" (which would elicit only a minor, forgettable detail), the teacher asks, "What do think was going through Sarah's mind when this accident occurred?" or "Was there anything that could have prevented the accident?" These more authentic questions tap a deeper level of student response to and interpretation of the incident.

When students are engaged in more authentic discourse, their thought and language becomes more sophisticated; they become more versatile at expressing their reactions to the material; they develop greater independence of response, since they're not focused simply on coming up with expected answers. All of these results, taken together, can empower students intellectually, and that empowerment leads inevitably to higher achievement and a desire to learn more.

OVERVIEW OF BOOK

The strategies included here were chosen because of their widespread applicability: They are useful across a wide range of subject areas, and most can be used at any grade level, K-12, though some may need to be modified to suit the ages of the students. They are purposely presented as notes rather than as scripted lesson plans so that each teacher, though adhering to the basic principles, can tailor the strategy to his or her needs.

Each strategy is divided into six major sections:

Strategy Overview Answers the question *What is it?* In this section you will find a brief overview of the strategy.

Instructional Benefits Answers the question *Why use it?* Here you will find several reasons to use the strategy.

Before, During, After ... Anytime Answers *When do I use it?* You will find here at what point to use the strategy in a lesson.

Strategy Step-by-Step Answers *What do I do?* This section provides an in-depth explanation of how to teach the strategy.

Strategy in Action Here you will find suggestions for implementing the strategy in your classroom and across the curriculum.

Sharing and Reflection Ideas for ways to cooperate with colleagues to refine and review your use of a particular strategy and reflect on its effectiveness are offered in the section. Such cooperation helps encourage authentic discourse.

We suggest that you read through the strategies to familiarize yourself with them. Then, go back and choose one strategy to learn. Plan a lesson and try it with your students. Reflect on the lesson. (You may want to keep a teacher journal for this purpose.) Ask yourself how it went. What could you do the next time to make it a better lesson? Then, plan another lesson using the same strategy. Use the strategy often until you are comfortable with it. Then, choose another strategy. Go through the same process. Then choose another strategy. Continue trying new strategies until you have built up a powerful repertoire.

The strategies are most effective if students are allowed to work in pairs or small groups (no more than four or five per group). Introduce and model the strategy to the whole class, but have them move quickly into their smaller groups. This allows for more purposeful dialogue and provides opportunities for all students to be involved and to participate.

A critical aspect of these strategies is the extended periods of discussion engaged in by students. For example, when working with an anticipation guide, students may read over the guide, make their choices, and then work with a partner discussing each question and comparing answers and discussing the reasons for their choices. Then the entire class would be involved in a teacher-led discussion about the most intriguing or interesting statements. After the discussion, students would read the pertinent article or chapter. The discussion is the key to students making connections, clarifying understandings, identifying misunderstandings, stimulating their interests, and gaining the motivation to read. Use the bibliography at the end of the book for further exploration of the concepts behind the strategies and the educational principles on which they are based. The article "Teaching for Intelligence: Parameters for Change" by Drs. Eric J. Cooper and Daniel U. Levine is presented here as an appendix for use by classroom teachers and administrators alike to begin a dialogue that will "bridge the gap between policy and good implementation."

THINKING STRATEGIES

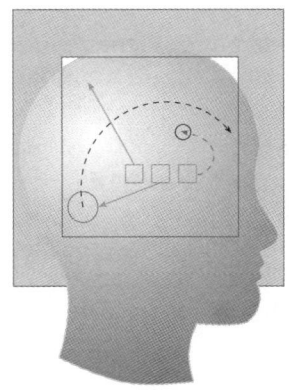

ANALOGIES

STRATEGY-AT-A-GLANCE

STRATEGY OVERVIEW
An analogy is a way of stating a relationship between things. Studying and creating analogies can help students develop personal understanding of the various ways things can be related to one another. Tadpole is to frog as kitten is to cat is an example of an analogy. Analogies can also be represented in the following way:

> Lincoln : president :: Henry VIII : king

which is the standard convention for identifying an analogy and is a kind of shorthand way to express that Lincoln is to president as Henry VIII is to king.

INSTRUCTIONAL BENEFITS
- ❏ helps develop student understanding of the nature of various kinds of relationships
- ❏ refines students' understanding of the specific vocabulary and concepts that are used in the analogies
- ❏ develops higher-order thinking abilities in students
- ❏ expands student vocabulary

BEFORE, DURING, AFTER . . . ANYTIME
- ❏ before a lesson or unit to introduce vocabulary and concepts
- ❏ after a lesson or unit to refine and extend vocabulary and concepts
- ❏ anytime as an enjoyable thinking exercise

Strategy Step-by-Step

The steps described below are best done in the sequence given here, but you may want to take several days or more to go through all the steps.

1. Have students brainstorm pairs of words that are related or associated in some way. Examples follow:

day	night
mother	daughter
wheel	bicycle
cake	frosting
bird	beak
acorn	oak

2. Have students state the relationship between the items in each pair. Building on the example above

day/night:	Day is the opposite of night.
wheel/bicycle:	A wheel is part of a bicycle.
cake/frosting:	Frosting is something that goes on top of cake.
acorn/oak:	An oak grows from an acorn.

3. Choosing analogous pairs that will likely be the easiest with which to work, have students think of other pairs that are related in the same way and list those alongside the pairs ordered in the same way.

day/night:	up/down, cold/hot, front/back
cake/frosting:	toast/jam, wall/paint, hair/hairspray
wheel/bicycle:	leg/chair, eraser/pencil, bristle/brush

4. Model for students how to show the relationships using the conventions of a formal statement of analogy. Make sure students understand that the ordering of the items on each side of the "equation" is important.

    cake : frosting :: toast : jam (NOT cake : frosting : : jam : toast)

    wheel : bicycle :: leg : chair (NOT wheel : bicycle :: chair : leg)

5. To reinforce the kind of thinking that's required for analogies, have students also write out how the items are related.

    cake : frosting :: toast : jam

    Cake is covered by frosting as toast is covered by jam.

    wheel : bicycle :: leg : chair

    A wheel is part of a bicycle as a leg is part of a chair.

6. Give students analogies with one term missing and have them work in pairs or groups to complete the analogy and state the nature of the relationship.

   convertible : car :: yacht : _____ (boat)

   Relationship—specific type of a general category of items

   envelope : letter :: backpack : _____ (books or other items)

   Relationship—container, contents

7. When students understand how to complete analogies, have them work in teams to make up new ones to offer as challenges to the whole class.

Strategy in Action

Have students work in teams to create analogies with words from a completed science or social studies unit. Each team can present their creations as incomplete analogies for the rest of the class to solve. Analogies can also be used in drawing relationships between mathematical concepts.

　　　　square : perimeter :: circle : circumference

　　　　sum : addition :: dividend : division

Sharing and Reflection

❏ Team up with a colleague to teach the respective classes how to solve and create analogies, and have them create incomplete analogies for the other class to solve. Compare notes on how your respective classes responded. Discuss how well their analogies reflect good thinking and an understanding of concepts being taught.

❏ Note in your teacher journal: How do students respond to this way of reviewing learned information? How insightful or inventive are their analogies? What might you do to improve the activity the next time?

❏ Have students create analogies regularly over a period of several weeks or months. Keep samples of their work and review them regularly. Do you see improvement over time in the quality and sophistication of their analogies? Keep the samples to use when you introduce the activity to next year's class.

Tips and Hints

- ❏ As a morning warm-up activity, put one or two incomplete analogies on the board for students to solve. After a time, invite students to submit analogies for this purpose, and use theirs often.
- ❏ After students are experienced at creating analogies, have them publish a booklet of incomplete analogies (with an answer key) and donate it to the school library or publish it on the school or district Web site.

ANTICIPATION GUIDE

STRATEGY-AT-A-GLANCE

STRATEGY OVERVIEW
An anticipation guide is a set of statements about a unit of expository material. The material may be a text, an audio tape, a film, or an electronic multimedia presentation. Students agree or disagree with the statements presented in the material, discussing and debating the relative merits of the statements. Then they turn to the material to get more information. Students then discuss the statements again and talk about how their thinking has changed.

INSTRUCTIONAL BENEFITS
- ❏ activates prior knowledge
- ❏ arouses curiosity about the topic
- ❏ stimulates high-level thinking
- ❏ promotes active involvement
- ❏ helps students set purposes for learning

BEFORE, DURING, AFTER . . . ANYTIME
- ❏ before reading, listening to, or viewing material to introduce the topic
- ❏ after or at the end of a lesson, present the guide again to check understanding and provide closure

Strategy Step-by-Step

1. Write several statements with which students are invited to agree or disagree based on information presented in the material. Include statements that will cause students to speculate and form hypotheses they can test. An anticipation guide that might be used in the elementary

grades is the birds' nests example shown below. In the primary grades, several sentences can be put on a large chart, read aloud by the teacher, and discussed by the whole class. In middle school or high school, a handout might be used with early Chicago as the topic.

BIRDS' NESTS

Student Directions:
Read the following sentences about birds' nests. Put an A in front of the sentence if you <u>agree</u> with it. Put a D in front of it if you <u>disagree</u> with it.

___ 1. Birds use grass to build their nests.
___ 2. Some birds use other birds' nests.
___ 3. Male and female birds build nests together.
___ 4. If the eggs get cold, they will not hatch.
___ 5. Mother birds sit on their nests all day.

EARLY CHICAGO

Student Directions: Decide if you agree (mark with an A) or disagree (mark with a D) with these statements about early Chicago. Put an A or D in front of each one to show what you think.

___1. Chicago had about 50,000 settlers in 1835.
___2. Muddy streets were a major problem in Chicago in 1850.
___3. The city's early growth was related to the Erie Canal.
___4. An early city law held the price of eight ounces of wine to twenty-five cents.
___5. The first permanent theater was established in 1837.

2. Before students read, listen to, or view the material, have them work in small groups to discuss the items and decide on their responses, then share their thinking with the whole class. Ask "Why do you think so?" frequently to encourage students to explain their reasoning. Be sure not to let students know who's right so they'll keep thinking and talking about the material. Also, probe their existing knowledge more deeply. For instance, if students say they think the Erie Canal was related to the growth of Chicago, ask them when and where they think the Erie Canal was built, who might have used it, and in what way that use might have influenced growth in Chicago. By pressing students (gently and with good humor) to search for connections and draw tentative conclusions, even when they're not sure if they're right, you will help them use what they know to assimilate the new information.

3. Have students turn to the material to confirm or revise their ideas. Then have them return to their anticipation guides and discuss the statements again in light of what they've learned. Have them cite evidence from the material to support their revisions.

4. Because an anticipation guide is used as an introduction to a body of material or a unit of instruction, you will need to spend time discussing important points, developing key concepts, and having students reread or study the material for other purposes.

5. In bringing the lesson to a close, ask one or more wrap-up questions such as the following:

    "What was the most interesting thing you learned?"

    "What was the most surprising thing you learned?"

    "How would you summarize what you learned?"

    "What questions do you have at this point?"

Strategy in Action

Use an anticipation guide to introduce a new topic in science as in the example above, "Birds' Nests," and in social studies as shown in the "Early Chicago" example. Language arts teachers can employ the strategy with biographical material.

Sharing and Reflection

❏ To show this strategy to colleagues, give them an anticipation guide that you've already used with your students. Have your colleagues fill out the guide, discuss their responses, and read the material. Then tell them how your own students responded.

❏ Work with another teacher to write an anticipation guide that each of you can use. After teaching the lesson to your classes, compare notes. Then share experiences and reflections with other colleagues. Observe how the students respond to the use of anticipation guides. Which statements provoke lively debate? Which ones don't work very well? What conclusions can you draw? How will you do things differently next time?

Tips and Hints

❏ Use anticipation guides with two different lessons in order to compare results. In the first, have students respond to the items individually and then discuss as a whole class. In the second, have students work in groups first and then have groups share their thinking. Is there any difference in the students' responses or in their interest in the activity?

❏ Try different kinds of items on anticipation guides to see which ones result in the best discussions. For instance, sometimes use factual statements that sound like true-false items (Chicago had about 50,000 settlers in 1835) and sometimes use statements of opinion (Early Chicago had the best opportunity for young people of any city of its time). Which of the two types of statements elicits the most fruitful and interesting discussion?

CUBING

STRATEGY-AT-A-GLANCE

STRATEGY OVERVIEW
Cubing is a writing-thinking activity that encourages students to explore meanings of a given object, concept, or phenomenon from six dimensions. It is a means for the teacher to inquire of students as well as a means for students to inquire of themselves what they already know or think they know about a topic. The stimulus for thinking is a cube that has six different writing prompts, one on each face. Students do a series of six focused freewritings on a specific topic, responding to each of the six prompts in turn.

INSTRUCTIONAL BENEFITS
- ❏ helps students think about a topic from multiple perspectives
- ❏ advances writing fluency
- ❏ develops flexibility in thinking
- ❏ encourages students to learn from each other by listening to each other's writing
- ❏ promotes students' independent use and further application

BEFORE, DURING, AFTER . . . ANYTIME
- ❏ before a lesson or unit to activate prior knowledge about key concepts and to set purposes for learning
- ❏ before a lesson as a pre-writing activity to generate ideas
- ❏ anytime as a concept-development strategy
- ❏ anytime to develop writing fluency and flexible thinking
- ❏ after a lesson or unit to review and rethink information

Strategy Step-by-Step

1. Decide how many small groups will be formed, and prepare enough cubes so that each group will have one. Make cubes by folding sturdy paper or by re-purposing large wooden or plastic cubes.

2. Put labels on the faces of the cubes, one label per face as follows:

describe	analyze
compare	apply
associate	argue for or against

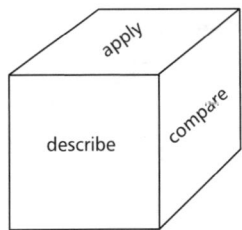

3. Organize the class into groups and give each group a cube. Announce the topic and tell students they'll be doing freewriting to explore the topic from different perspectives, as shown on the faces of their cubes. Let students examine the cubes for a few minutes and explain any prompts that they may not understand. Then have them turn the cubes so that "describe" appears on the top face.

4. Tell students to do a focused freewriting to describe the topic (see the freewriting strategy, pages 17–19). Assure them that there's no "right" thing to say and that they should write whatever comes to mind to help them describe the topic. Have all students begin at the same time and write for five minutes (or longer if desired).

5. When the time is up, have students take turns reading their freewritings to the members of their group. By listening to each other, students will enhance their understanding of the topic and get a sense of how the others in the group are thinking about it. Such sharing also provides a short break before the next focused freewriting.

6. Have each group turn its cube so that "compare" appears on top. Have students begin focused freewriting to compare the topic with any other thing. Again, have students read these new writings aloud in their groups when the writing time is up. Continue this way until students have written in response to all the prompts on the cube.

7. For closure, lead a discussion with the whole class to get students thinking about how shifting their perspectives affected their writing and their understanding of the topic. Some questions that stimulate discussion include:
   - Which writing was easiest? Why?
   - Which writing did you enjoy the most?
   - Which writing was the hardest? Why?
   - Did any of the prompts make you think about the topic in a whole new way?
   - In what ways has your understanding of the topic changed or improved?

Strategy in Action

Have individual students do cubing with a character from literature as the topic. Or assign a different character to each small group. Have students share their writings within their groups and with the whole class.

Try a variety of objects, concepts, and phenomena as topics for cubing. Following are a few ideas:

Concrete Objects	Abstract Concepts	Phenomena or Events
pencil	freedom	thunderstorms
television	happiness	the common cold
fresh apple	compassion	a school ceremony
backpack	duty	a sporting event

Sharing and Reflection

- ❏ Use Cubing when another teacher uses it with his or her class. Compare notes on how well students responded, and read over the papers together.
- ❏ Demonstrate Cubing to some colleagues by having them do it with a concept such as "teacher" or "student." Tell them how you have used cubing with your students.
- ❏ Discuss the following questions with your colleagues after you have used the strategy:
  - How does this activity affect your students' ability to think, talk, and write about literary characters?
  - How did students respond? Do you think cubing helps your students prepare to write?

Tips and Hints

- ❏ When students have done cubing in small groups several times, have them make their own individual cubes and do the same activity independently. Encourage students to use cubing to generate ideas before writing or to review things they've learned about.
- ❏ Show students a familiar object, such as a table fork, a plastic tube, or a piece of clothing, or give each group a different object. Have students do cubing with the object as the topic and then write an essay about the object.
- ❏ First, have students write about a concept from a unit they've just finished. Use a simple prompt such as "Write what you know about ___." Save the papers. The next day, have students cube the same key concept. When they've finished, have them again write what they know about the concept, using the same prompt. Compare the sets of papers. Have students compare them, too, and discuss how cubing affected their second attempt.

FRAME PARAGRAPHS

STRATEGY-AT-A-GLANCE

STRATEGY OVERVIEW
A frame paragraph is a paragraph that contains only structural elements and is used as a guide for student writing. Students fill in the frame with their own ideas to complete the paragraph.

> **A FRAME PARAGRAPH:**
> My favorite television program is _____. I like the program for several reasons. First, _____. Second, _____. Third, _____. Those are the reasons I think _____ is such a great program.

INSTRUCTIONAL BENEFITS
- ❏ models how to organize and write paragraphs
- ❏ helps students learn to develop their own paragraphs more fully
- ❏ highlights the way different kinds of paragraphs are organized

BEFORE, DURING, AFTER . . . ANYTIME
- ❏ anytime when modeling paragraph development
- ❏ as a preliminary step to having students generate their own paragraphs
- ❏ anytime as a language arts writing practice exercise

Strategy Step-by-Step

You will probably want to model the use of the frame paragraph before having students use it on their own. Put a frame paragraph on an overhead transparency or on the board and add ideas or information to show students how to build up the paragraph. After one or more such demonstration sessions, try these steps:

1. Give students the same frame that you modeled and have them create their own paragraphs with it.
2. Give students a different frame based on the same organizational pattern as the first. For instance, after giving students the sample paragraph shown above, try one like this to give them more practice with the same organizational pattern:

Frame Paragraph

I'm very much in favor of _____. Here are my reasons for having this opinion. First, _____. Next, _____. Finally, _____. Those are the reasons I'm in favor of _____.

Have students share their paragraphs so they can see how the same frame can be transformed into a variety of different paragraphs.

3. Have students work with other frame paragraphs that are based on different organizational patterns. For instance, if you've focused on opinions supported by reasons, you may want to have students work next with chronological order, comparison or contrast, or cause-effect patterns.
4. After a round of practice as described above, post examples of completed paragraphs in the room to which students can refer when they write without the use of frames.

Strategy in Action

Have students write a paragraph that explains how to do a task that involves several steps. Collect their first drafts and put them aside. Next, introduce a

frame paragraph with a chronological-order pattern and have students use it in writing an explanation of a different multi-step task. Then return students' first paragraphs to them for revision in light of what they learned from using the frame paragraph as a writing guide. Are students able to make substantive revisions to their drafts based on what they learned?

Sharing and Reflection

Focus on frame-paragraph writing activities for a week or more. Then have students return to writing without these aids. Do you notice any differences in the quality of their writing before and after the time spent on frame paragraphs?

Tips and Hints

❑ Introduce a frame paragraph of any organizational pattern. After students have written one or more paragraphs with the frame as a guide, have them skim periodicals for examples of other writers' paragraphs that follow the same kind of pattern, then compare them with their own.

❑ Find a paragraph in a newspaper or magazine that illustrates good adherence to a pattern of organization. Prepare a frame from that paragraph for students to use as a guide. When they've written their own paragraphs, have them compare theirs with the original paragraph from the periodical.

❑ Have students keep completed frame paragraphs in their writing notebooks and use them as reminders or models when they write.

FREEWRITING

STRATEGY-AT-A-GLANCE

STRATEGY OVERVIEW
Freewriting is a strategy that helps writers get started writing and builds writing fluency. Students are asked to write steadily without stopping and without worrying about mechanics for a predetermined period of time, usually somewhere between two and ten minutes. Freewriting helps students collect their thoughts and explore associations and reactions. It can be used as a prewriting activity or as a way to determine how much a student knows about a given topic. Freewriting can be used in learning logs and journals or as a way to generate ideas and thoughts that do not have to be shared.

INSTRUCTIONAL BENEFITS
- ❏ increases writing fluency
- ❏ helps students get started on a writing assignment
- ❏ generates ideas for writing
- ❏ provides an opportunity to think about what students want to say
- ❏ builds confidence in writing
- ❏ accesses prior knowledge
- ❏ helps students review what they have learned

BEFORE, DURING, AFTER . . . ANYTIME
- ❏ anytime to generate ideas for future writing
- ❏ before writing as an activity to generate ideas
- ❏ as an introduction to a concept to access prior knowledge

Strategy Step-by-Step

Explain the purpose of freewriting to your students, telling them your goals for introducing it as a strategy. Model the process by doing a freewriting on

the board while they watch. Make sure that each student has paper or a journal in which to do their freewriting.

Student Guidelines for Unfocused Freewriting

1. Write for three to five minutes (or longer if you wish). Write whatever is on your mind.

2. Don't stop writing for any reason. Go steadily without rushing. If you can't think of something to write, write "Thinking" or another word until the ideas start to flow again.

3. Don't stop to look back, to cross something out, or to wonder how to spell.

4. If you can't think of a word or spelling, just use a line or write, "I can't think of it."

5. Don't worry about how your writing sound or looks, just keep writing until time is up.

For focused freewriting, proceed as above but announce the topic. Students are required to stay with the topic for the allotted time. (See the cubing strategy (pages 10–13) for a technique to facilitate focused freewriting.)

Strategy in Action

Use as a means for evaluating prior student knowledge of any content area topic.

Sharing and Reflection

- ❏ Plan a lesson together with a colleague and have your classes do a focused freewriting on a lesson's topic. Compare the writing from the two classes. What did you learn about your students by doing this activity?
- ❏ Have students do a focused freewriting about a specific topic. Then have them discuss the topic. Ask students what effects freewriting had on their ability to talk about the topic.
- ❏ After completing a unit of study, ask students to do a focused freewriting about the topic. Have them discuss whether the freewriting helped to clarify their thoughts and whether it led to additional questions?
- ❏ Start a journal of your own and do five minutes or more of freewriting every day for two weeks. What do you notice about your own writing? Share your reflections with your students.
- ❏ After introducing freewriting to students, have them do unfocused freewriting for several weeks. Do you notice any difference in the time they spend writing or the amount of writing they are doing?

GRAPHIC ORGANIZERS

STRATEGY-AT-A-GLANCE

STRATEGY OVERVIEW

A graphic organizer is a scheme for arranging information on a page so that the relationships among the concepts are made clear visually. For instance, a causal relationship might be shown with an arrow pointing from the cause to the effect, or subordinate details might be shown radiating from a main idea like spokes from the center of a wheel. For some learners, information is easier to process if the ideas are arranged graphically instead of in a linear fashion as is the case with traditional outlines, lists, or pages of notes. For most learners, such visual displays can be aids to comprehension and retention of information.

There are many different types of graphic organizers. The one to choose depends on the kind of relationships that are inherent in the material or the relationship on which students are asked to focus.

INSTRUCTIONAL BENEFITS

- ❏ helps students understand relationships among ideas
- ❏ refines and extends comprehension of information
- ❏ helps students see learned information from new perspectives
- ❏ encourages students to try them as an independent study strategy

BEFORE, DURING, AFTER . . . ANYTIME

- ❏ before a lesson or unit to activate prior knowledge and set purposes for learning
- ❏ during instruction as a way of organizing new information and relating it to previously known information
- ❏ after learning to review and restate the information
- ❏ anytime to establish a conceptual framework for making connections among concepts

Strategy Step-by-Step

1. Guide students to construct one or more graphic organizers with you to show them this way of displaying information. Provide the visual structure, and use material from a recent lesson or topic of discussion so that students will be familiar with the vocabulary and concepts and can concentrate on seeing the relationships. Following are some examples:

Venn Diagram

Have students write a brief account to compare and contrast two things, such as historical figures, kinds of plants or animals, literary selections. Collect their papers and put them aside. Then, working with the whole class, use a Venn diagram to guide students in comparing and contrasting the same two things. Return the students' accounts and have them revise, using the ideas from the graphic organizer. Have students discuss the ways in which the graphic organizer helped them improve their writing.

Example 1: Comparing and Contrasting Fictional Characters

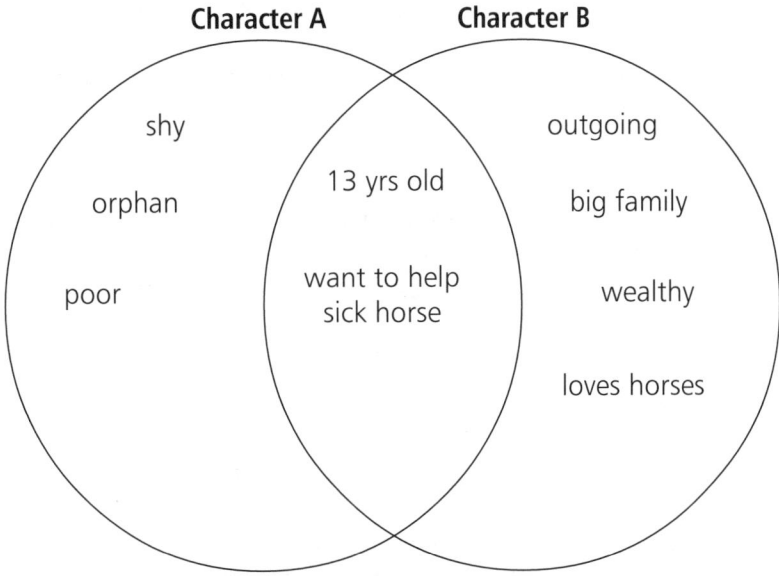

SkyLight Professional Development

GRAPHIC ORGANIZERS 21

T-Chart

Use a T-chart to help students clarify, compare, and prioritize.

Example 2: Main Ideas and Details

Doubles tennis is fun	Doubles tennis teaches cooperation
more people playing	must work with your partner
can be a faster game	set up shots for partner
take turns at net and back	you're BOTH responsible

2. After you've constructed a few graphic organizers with students, put them in small groups, give each group a blank organizer to go with a reading assignment (or other learning material), and have them work together to fit the information into the structure. Have groups share their work and discuss any differences in their completed organizers. Do this several times until students are comfortable using the organizing structures you provide.

3. After reading a literary selection or a section from a content-area textbook, have students work in small groups to decide how they could organize the information graphically. Have groups share their organizers and discuss the kind of thinking that went into their decisions. Do this several times with different texts.

4. These three steps will provide students with a good introduction to using graphic organizers. To encourage students to refine their use of this strategy, use it as a whole-class activity for introducing and reviewing units of instruction; have small groups use organizers in brainstorming activities; and encourage individuals to use them for generating thoughts before writing, taking notes, and reviewing learning.

Strategy in Action

Graphic organizers be used in just about every type of content area. At the end of a unit, or when students have completed a reading assignment, have them work in small groups to summarize the ideas in a graphic organizer. Provide a blank organizer or have students construct their own, depending on how familiar they are with the strategy. Have groups share their work.

Sharing and Reflection

❑ Take turns in a small group of colleagues to show the kinds of graphic organizers you use with your students and explain how you use the strategy. Share tips and discuss other ways you might make use of the strategy.

❑ Plan a lesson with a colleague in which you'll both use a graphic organizer, having students respond as a whole class or in small groups. Compare notes on how well your students did, and show each other the completed organizers. Then share your experiences and reflections with other colleagues.

❑ Note in a course diary or journal your reflections on the following: How effective do you think this strategy was for helping students review and summarize the material? What might you do differently the next time you use the strategy? Why?

I-SEARCH REPORTS

STRATEGY-AT-A-GLANCE

STRATEGY OVERVIEW
An I-Search report is an original piece of expository writing that's based on a question a student poses and then answers by researching information. The research may include interviews and observations as well as use of print and electronic sources. Such reports are ordinarily written in the first person and are usually conversational in tone and approach.

INSTRUCTIONAL BENEFITS
- allows report writing to grow from students' own interests and purposes
- develops research and reporting skills
- stimulates interesting, original expository writing
- prepares students for writing more formal research reports that are based on reading
- refines and extends general writing abilities

BEFORE, DURING, AFTER . . . ANYTIME
- anytime as a language arts writing assignment
- anytime as a writing assignment in content areas (having students report on questions of interest that relate to units of study)
- as a preliminary step to having students write formal research papers

Strategy Step-by-Step

You will probably want to give students several days or more to complete the sequence.

1. Students formulate questions based on their own personal interests, which are usually related to immediate concerns and pursuits. For instance, a student who has just obtained a new pet will be interested in learning about the animal and finding out how to care for it. Following are some interests and questions to illustrate the kind of response you might expect from students:

   - We're going to Yellowstone National Park this summer. What things can I see and do there?
   - I like soccer. When did the game start? Where? Who's the best player today?
   - I want to have a vegetable garden. How do I do that?
   - I want to be a computer engineer. What kind of training do I need?

   As students formulate their questions, help them narrow questions that are very broad or add related questions as you see fit. For instance, the question above about when soccer was first played is enhanced with the two additional questions, while the one about how to grow a vegetable garden is too broad. (Better: What do I need to know to grow good tomatoes?)

2. Have students work in pairs or groups to make lists of possible sources of information. Provide suggestions and help as needed, reminding students that sources may include persons who know about their topic, organizations that can be reached by phone, television programs, and Internet sites as well as books. Students should be encouraged to use non-book sources as much as possible for this kind of reporting so that they see how "research" can involve more than looking things up in reference books.

3. Students conduct their searches by gathering information and taking notes over the course of several days or longer. Have them keep their questions with them as they search. If they have more than one question, have them organize their notes by question.

4. When students are ready to write their drafts, have them write in the first person, as if they are simply talking to someone about what questions they had, listing sources they consulted to find the answers, and telling what they discovered.

> I'm interested in having a vegetable garden, so I started by thinking about tomatoes. My mom told me that a lady on our block grows tomatoes every year, so I went to talk to her. She told me to start with little tomato plants because they are a lot easier than starting with seeds.

> There's a lot more to being a computer engineer than I thought. I wanted to know what training I needed, so I talked to two men and a woman who work where my dad works. They're all computer engineers and they all told me...

When students adopt such a conversational tone, they naturally write what they learned in their own words. This can help them when they later report information they obtain from reading.

5. Have students meet in small groups to help each other revise their drafts to improve clarity of expression, use of supporting details, and anything else on which you want them to focus.

6. Have students publish their I-Search reports by posting them around the classroom, in the hallway, or on the school's or district's Web site. You may also want to have students present their findings orally. Keep copies of their reports to use as examples for the next time you use the strategy or to share with colleagues.

Strategy in Action

I-Search reports can be used to stimulate report writing in any content discipline.

Sharing and Reflection

- ❏ Tell interested colleagues how you use I-Search reports. Show them examples of your students' work and ask them to comment. How do their responses compare to yours?
- ❏ Compare your students' writing in I-Search reports with their work when they write more traditional reports. Do you notice any differences? Do students respond any differently to I-Search reports in comparison to more traditional reports?

Tips and Hints

- ❏ Establish a Question Wall in your room where students can write interesting questions at any time. When it's time for an I-Search assignment, have students mine the Question Wall for questions to use. As students become familiar with the I-Search process, do you notice any change in the quantity and quality of contributions to the Question Wall?
- ❏ Maintain an ongoing list of questions that students use for their I-Search papers—for your own records and to review with students periodically. Have students evaluate the questions they asked at different points in the year and encourage them to comment on how their attitude toward asking such questions has changed. How do their assessments match yours?
- ❏ When students are familiar with I-Search reports, challenge them to pose questions that they consider more difficult than usual (but that are still grounded in their genuine interests). How do they respond? What happens when they go in search of answers? Do you notice any change in the quality of their reports?

ary # IMITATION WRITING

STRATEGY-AT-A-GLANCE

STRATEGY OVERVIEW
Imitation writing involves writing to follow (imitate) the structure or pattern of a model. The model can be a sentence, a paragraph, a poem, or some other piece of writing that's either selected from an existing work or composed by the teacher. There are four steps students follow in the imitation process:
1. Read the model carefully.
2. Copy the model word for word.
3. Substitute synonyms for as many words as possible.
4. Write on a different topic using the same syntactical structure as the model.

INSTRUCTIONAL BENEFITS
- improves writing versatility and expressiveness
- increases understanding of sentence structure
- refines reading comprehension ability
- develops reading and writing vocabularies
- establishes a base for teaching grammar concepts

BEFORE, DURING, AFTER . . . ANYTIME
- any time daily or weekly as a regular writing activity
- before writing as a warm-up exercise
- before students revise a piece of writing
- as an introduction to a grammar lesson
- after students read to savor the language of literature

Strategy Step-by-Step

1. Write the model or choose one from an existing source. You'll want a model that's challenging but not too difficult for your students. Short, simple sentences or poetic rhythms are appropriate for primary-grade students or for students who haven't done this activity before. More complicated sentences, paragraphs, and poems are appropriate for older or more experienced students. When you've selected a sentence, try it out yourself first to see how it works. Some sentences are better than others for this activity.

2. Model the four steps in the process for the whole class, thinking aloud and composing while they watch.

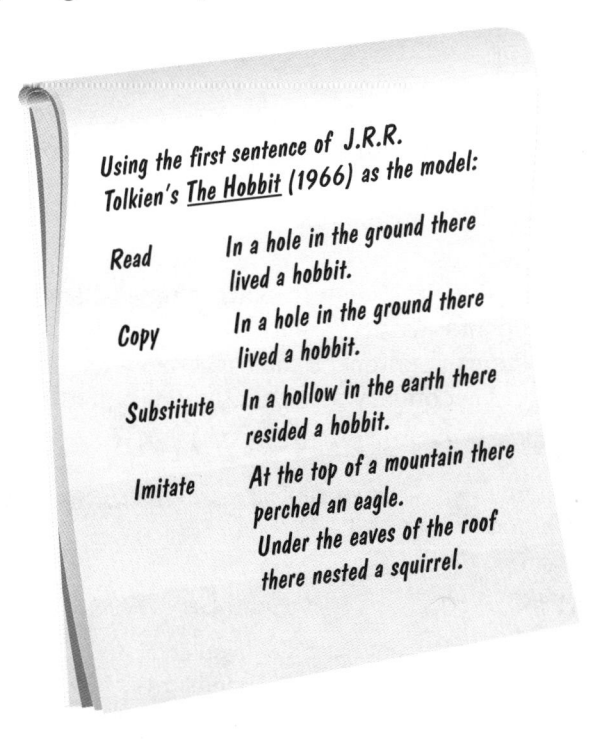

Using the first sentence of J.R.R. Tolkien's *The Hobbit* (1966) as the model:

Read	In a hole in the ground there lived a hobbit.
Copy	In a hole in the ground there lived a hobbit.
Substitute	In a hollow in the earth there resided a hobbit.
Imitate	At the top of a mountain there perched an eagle.
	Under the eaves of the roof there nested a squirrel.

3. Invite students to provide other examples that adhere to the syntactical pattern (in the above instance—two prepositional phrases, adverb "there," verb, subject). Accept all attempts, but point out any deviations

from the model and help students revise these to better match the model.

4. Have students work individually, in pairs, or in small groups to compose more sentences in imitation of the model. Have students share their sentences with the whole class by writing them on the board or on overhead transparencies so that everyone can see the sentences as well as hear them.

5. If you wish, use the model and the sentences the students create to develop grammar concepts. For instance, you could use *The Hobbit* example to teach prepositional phrases and to show students how subjects sometimes follow verbs in sentences.

Strategy in Action

In the primary grades, books with simple, predictable text are excellent models for imitation writing. For instance, books like *Brown Bear, Brown Bear, What Do You See?* (1992) by Bill Martin, Jr. can be used as a model for students to create their own books that follow the same syntactic and rhyming patterns.

In the upper grades, modeling sentences from novels, short stories, or folktales can stretch students' writing abilities in interesting and enjoyable ways. Following are two excerpt sentences that have been used successfully with upper elementary and secondary students to elicit imitation writing.

From Philip Sendak's *In Grandpa's House* (1985)

> Ours was a beautiful town. It had a central marketplace, and every Thursday the peasants came to buy and sell.

From Peter S. Beagle's *The Last Unicorn* (1991)

> The unicorn lived in a lilac wood, and she lived all alone. She was very old, though she did not know it, and she was no longer the careless color of sea foam, but rather the color of snow falling on a moonlit night.

Imitation writing can also be applied in social studies units using sentences from famous historical speeches, such as Abraham Lincoln's *Gettysburg Address* ("Four-score and seven years ago…"), Franklin Roosevelt's first inaugural address ("We have nothing to fear but fear itself"), or the "I Have a Dream" speech Martin Luther King delivered in front of the Lincoln Memorial in 1963.

Sharing and Reflection

- ❏ Work with another teacher to choose a sentence that you can both use for imitation writing. Compare notes on how your students responded and on the sentences they created. Then share your experiences and reflections with other colleagues.
- ❏ Introduce your colleagues to imitation writing by giving them a sentence to imitate. Have them discuss the kind of reading and thinking they had to do in order to write a good imitation. Invite them to try the same activity with their own students. Get together again to compare notes.

Tips and Hints

- ❏ As a model for imitation writing, choose a sentence from a story you're reading with your class. Keep a copy of the imitation sentences your students create. Do this regularly for a few weeks with new sentences. Then give them the first sentence to try again. Compare their two attempts.
- ❏ Have students work in groups to choose a sentence and do two or three imitations of it. Have groups share their examples with the rest of the class. What do you notice about the sentences they choose? How well were they able to write imitations?
- ❏ Choose a sentence that illustrates a specific concept in grammar or a rule of punctuation. After students do imitations, ask them to study a few of their examples (the ones that are successful imitations) and state the concept or rule they imitated in their own words.

9

JOURNALS

STRATEGY-AT-A-GLANCE

STRATEGY OVERVIEW
A journal is an individual notebook in which a student writes freely. Journals can be used for private reflections, writing that others will read and respond to, recording observations, reflecting on recent learning, and other such purposes.

INSTRUCTIONAL BENEFITS
- ❏ increases writing fluency and comfort with writing
- ❏ helps students think of themselves as writers
- ❏ reinforces and enhances learning
- ❏ encourages students to reflect on what they are thinking and learning

BEFORE, DURING, AFTER . . . ANYTIME
- ❏ during a lesson to record notes, reactions, or reflective comments
- ❏ after or at the end of a lesson to summarize and reflect on learning
- ❏ anytime as a way to encourage students to record ideas, reactions, or questions, quotations, or other material they want to remember

Strategy Step-by-Step

1. Decide on the type of journal you want your students to keep. Several common types are described on the following pages.
2. Establish a journal-writing routine and stick to it. Set aside a time of day and a schedule (every day, every other day, once or twice a week) for journal writing and post it to remind yourself and students to do it.

3. Establish guidelines for using journals with your students. For example:
   - Write every day.
   - Write for at least fifteen minutes.
   - Write at least three sentences.
4. Provide each student with a journal. Journals can be as simple as several sheets of paper stapled together or can be booklets purchased from a store.
5. Plan time to have students share their entries and discuss or respond to one another's ideas.
6. Keep a journal yourself (writing in front of students regularly) and share its contents with your students.

Strategy in Action

The type of journal you choose to use in your classroom will depend upon the type of material with which you are working. Character journals, double-entry journals, reader response journals, and learning logs each provide unique opportunities for active learning and are discussed in detail below.

Character Journal

"A character journal is a written diary kept by a reader as he or she assumes the role of the main character as a book is read" (Hancock 1993, 1).

Guidelines for Teachers

1. Model one or more character-journal entries for the entire class before asking students to keep their own. Use books that have strong main characters, preferably about the same age as your students.
2. Read a chapter or two a day with or to your class. Then collaborate to write a journal entry in the character's "voice." Include a personal response (in a different color) after the character's entry.
3. After you and your class have kept a character response journal together for a while, have individuals keep their own. Provide a range of book titles and let students choose their own book and character. Or, the entire class can read the same book and choose characters from that book.

Guidelines for Students

1. Think about the character you have chosen. Where does the character live? What does the character look like? How does the character dress? What is your character doing, thinking, seeing?
2. Write each entry as you imagine the character would. Always include the date that the character would have used.
3. Write a journal entry for each chapter.
4. Write your personal thoughts after your character entry. Use two colors to write: one for the character's thoughts and feelings, one for your own.

Double-Entry Journal

A double-entry journal is used to keep two separate entries related to the same topic. It provides a way to combine what one knows (and feels) with what one is learning.

For response to reading

1. Have students divide a journal page into two columns.
2. In the left-hand column, students record information from the text, summaries of their reading, or quotations.
3. In the right-hand column, directly opposite the entries, students record personal responses to the information. These entries can be observations, feelings, reactions, questions, or their own interpretations.

For instruction

1. Provide questions or directions that tap students' prior knowledge. Students record these in the left-hand column.
2. After instruction, students record what they learned from reading and discussing the text in the right-hand column next to the relevant question or direction.

9

Examples of use in content areas

Math: In the left-hand column students record a problem. In the right-hand column they write the process for solving the problem.

Science: Observations go in the left-hand column. The right-hand column is for questions, hypotheses, or conclusions about the observations.

Double-Entry Journals

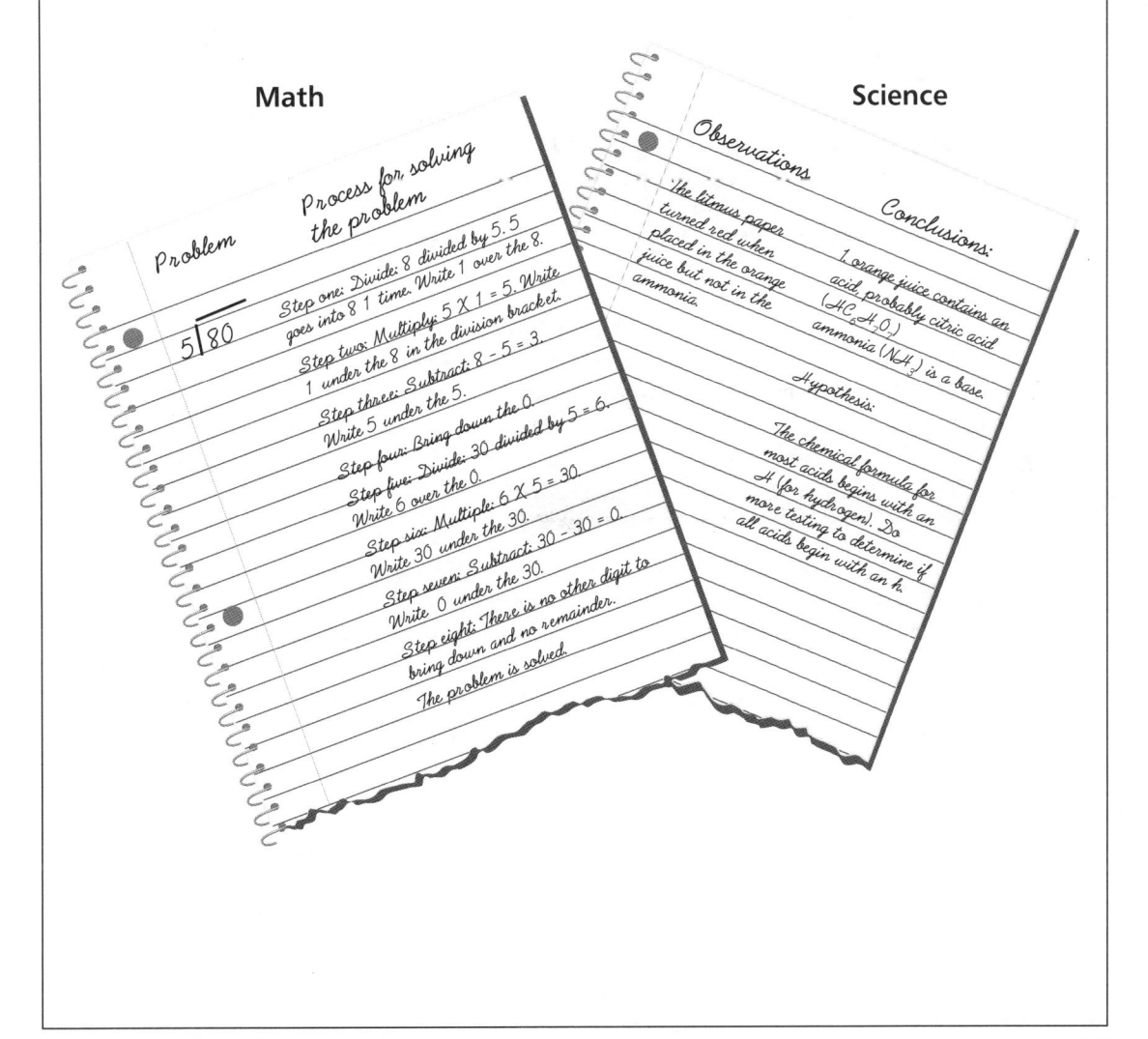

Math

Problem | Process for solving the problem

5)80

Step one: Divide: 8 divided by 5. 5 goes into 8 1 time. Write 1 over the 8.
Step two: Multiply: 5 X 1 = 5. Write 1 under the 8 in the division bracket.
Step three: Subtract: 8 - 5 = 3. Write 5 under the 5.
Step four: Bring down the 0.
Step five: Divide: 30 divided by 5 = 6. Write 6 over the 0.
Step six: Multiply: 6 X 5 = 30. Write 30 under the 30.
Step seven: Subtract: 30 - 30 = 0. Write 0 under the 30.
Step eight: There is no other digit to bring down and no remainder. The problem is solved.

Science

Observations | Conclusions:

The litmus paper turned red when placed in the orange juice but not in the ammonia.

1. orange juice contains an acid, probably citric acid ($HC_6H_7O_7$)
2. ammonia (NH_3) is a base.

Hypothesis:

The chemical formula for most acids begins with an H (for hydrogen). Do more testing to determine if all acids begin with an h.

Reader Response Journal

A reader response journal is used by students to reflect on what they are reading and to make connections to their own lives.

Guidelines for Teachers

1. Select a book with characters your students can relate to in some way.
2. With students, plan a schedule for reading and writing. Post the schedule and make sure everyone adheres to it.
3. Use questions like these to help students write:
   How did the story make you feel?
   Did this part remind you of anything you've experienced?
   Who is your favorite (least favorite) character? Why?
   What is your favorite part so far? Why?
   What do you think will happen next? Why?
   What has surprised you so far?
   Is there anyone in this story that reminds you of someone you know? Who? Why?
   How is the main character like you?
   How is the main character different from you?
   Do you agree or disagree with what the main character did? Why?
4. Plan times to discuss response journals.

Learning Log

Learning logs allow students to record what they have learned, react to new learning and learning situations, log observations, question, identify problems with their own learning, and dialogue with other students or the teacher.

In primary grades, students can start with drawing pictures and labeling them. More information can be drawn out through discussion.

Guidelines for Teachers

1. Select a content area in which to use learning logs.
2. Provide time for students to write in their logs frequently.
3. Guide students' entries with questions, for example:
   What did you learn today?
   Tell one new thing you learned in (math, science, social studies) today.
   What questions do you still have?
   Was there anything you didn't understand?
   Tell how you: solved a problem, reached a conclusion, figured something out.
4. Provide time for students to share their entries, discuss questions and concerns they have in common, and talk about the other ways they use their logs as an aid to learning.

Sharing and Reflection

❑ How does journal writing affect students' comprehension of stories, content-area texts, or other instructional materials? What effects do you think journals have on class discussions? How has that information affected your teaching?

❑ Team up with a colleague to use journals in the same way in your classes. Compare notes on how your students' use of journals affects their own comprehension and participation in discussions. Share what you've learned about maintaining the routine, keeping students motivated, and using the journals to assess your students' knowledge and progress.

Tips and Hints

❑ Keep a class character journal. Read a book aloud to your class. For the first two chapters, model by writing entries while students watch. Starting with the third chapter, have students contribute to the character journal.

❑ Introduce learning logs. Select a content area and introduce learning logs. After students have kept their learning logs for several days, start scheduling individual conferences to read entries with students and discuss the questions and other issues reflected in their journals.

KEY WORDS

STRATEGY-AT-A-GLANCE

STRATEGY OVERVIEW

This strategy helps get students ready to learn information from expository material. The teacher tells the students the topic, presents an array of key words from the text, and invites speculation and discussion on how the terms relate to the topic and to each other. Students form hypotheses, debate their ideas, then read the material to get more information. The material may be a content area text to read, a tape to listen to, a film to watch, or a multimedia presentation from a CD-ROM or an Internet source. Students then discuss what they have learned, returning to the key words to talk about how their thinking has changed.

INSTRUCTIONAL BENEFITS
- activates prior knowledge before reading, listening, viewing
- arouses curiosity about the topic
- stimulates high-level thinking
- promotes active involvement
- encourages students to set purposes for learning

BEFORE, DURING, AFTER . . . ANYTIME
- before reading, listening, or viewing to introduce a topic
- after or at the end of the lesson to check understanding and provide closure

Strategy Step-by-Step

1. From the expository material, select eight to fifteen terms that relate to the topic and that can be associated with each other in different ways. You can use almost any words or phrases, including names of people and

places, concrete objects or abstract concepts, and dates or other numbers. Include some terms you think students will have heard before, even if they don't know how to relate them to the topic, so that they will be able to generate some hypotheses. You don't need to include all the important concepts because this activity is used primarily for introducing the lesson. As an example, the following is a set of terms selected by one teacher from an article about kangaroos that the students were going to read.

Kangaroos

8 months	250	12 to 15
20 feet	lima beans	joey
boomer	mob	
tall grasses		

2. Ask students how they think the terms relate to the topic and, perhaps, to each other. Assure students that you don't expect them to have the right answers but that you want them to form the best hypotheses they can. If students are very hesitant, suggest that they make up a story about the topic that includes as many terms as possible, or tell them to just take the terms one at a time and decide what each one has to do with the topic, even if they need to guess.

3. Have students share ideas. Ask probing questions that encourage them to think carefully about their speculations, explain their reasoning, listen

to each other, and weigh the different perspectives that arise. Praise students for their thinking, but remain neutral about the accuracy of their statements so that they will not be overly concerned with guessing the right answers. Following are some good questions and responses to use at this point:

- That's an interesting idea. Why do you think so?
- What do the rest of you think of that idea?
- That's one way of looking at it. Does anyone have another way?
- What leads you to think that might be true?
- Why do you say that? What train of thought led you to that point?
- (Student X) thinks ___. Do you all agree? Why or why not?
- (Student X) thinks ___. If that's true, what are the implications?
- Is there any other way of looking at this?
- What else might we have neglected to consider?
- (Student X) and (Student Y) seem to have very different perspectives. Listen to each side carefully and decide if you agree with one of them or if you have yet another idea.

4. When you think the discussion has gone on long enough, have students turn to the material to get more information. After they complete it, have them first return to the key words and tell how they have revised their thinking in light of what they have learned. Have them cite evidence from the material to support their statements. Then discuss other concepts as needed. You may have students write a summary of what they have learned, using the original key words and any other important terms they want to include.

Strategy in Action

When you introduce a new topic in science or social studies, use the Key Word strategy with eight to ten words from the learning material. In science for example, the key words might relate to genetics. Have students decide which words relate to genetics and which do not. Then have students read the material to verify their choice.

Sharing and Reflection

- Work with another teacher to plan a key word strategy lesson that you both can use with your respective students. After you have each taught the lesson, get together to compare notes. Then share your experiences and reflections with other colleagues.
- Tell your colleagues about a time you tried the key word strategy with your students. Show the set of words you used and offer highlights of the discussion. Tell how your students responded, and share a few examples of their hypotheses and reasoning.
- When using the strategy to introduce a new topic in science or social studies, consider the following: How do the students respond to the different questions you ask? Which questions elicit the best response? Do any students respond in unexpected ways? What do you think accounts for the atypical responses?
- Use the key word strategy with two different lessons and compare the results. Is there any difference in the students' response? If so, what do you think accounts for the difference: the topic? the kinds of terms used in the set? the particular questions you asked? something else? A variation or further refinement would be to use the same key word strategy lesson with two different groups of students and compare the results. Is there any difference in the students' response? If so, what do you think accounts for the difference?

Tips and Hints

A variation for the primary grades is to select several words that are associated with the topic and a few that are not. Give students packets of note cards with one word on each card, and have them sort the cards into "yes" and "no" piles according to whether or not they think the words have to do with the topic. This activity stimulates the same kind of thinking as the regular approach but is somewhat easier. Students just need to make one decision for each word rather than deal with a variety of possible associations and combinations among the set of terms.

KWL

STRATEGY-AT-A-GLANCE

STRATEGY OVERVIEW
KWL is a strategy that can be used to develop comprehension through activating prior knowledge. According to Donna Ogle (1986), the originator of the strategy, KWL is best suited for use with expository texts. When using this strategy, students identify what they know (K), what they want to know (W), and what they have learned and still want to know (L) about a new unit, theme, or topic.

INSTRUCTIONAL BENEFITS
- activates students' prior knowledge and sets purposes for learning
- increases comprehension
- assesses students' prior knowledge
- identifies misconceptions about a topic
- encourages students to think about resources and strategies for gathering information
- stimulates interest in a topic

BEFORE, DURING, AFTER . . . ANYTIME
- before a lesson or unit to activate prior knowledge and set purposes for learning
- during instruction as a way of organizing new information and relating it to previously known information
- after learning to record new information
- after learning to brainstorm additional questions for later study

Strategy Step-by-Step

1. Before you introduce a new unit, theme, or topic, prepare a chart with three columns. Label the columns:

K What I **K**now	W What I **W**ant to Know	L What I **L**earned What I Still Want to Know

2. Introduce the new unit, theme, or topic. Display the KWL organizer on an overhead transparency or on a chart.

3. Begin by asking students to brainstorm what they know about the topic. When students make a contribution, ask them where or how they got their information, challenging students into higher levels of thinking.

4. Next, help students look for ways in which the brainstorming list can be reorganized into categories. Encourage students to look at the list and think about other categories represented in the list.

5. Record students responses on the chart under the column labeled K—*What I Know.*

6. Next, have students think about what they would like to know about the topic. Review the K—*What I Know* list to note gaps in knowledge, what information is missing, or disagreements about information. Record the questions students have under the column labeled W—*What I Want to Know.*

7. Leave the chart posted as you go through the unit, theme, or new concept.
8. At the end of a unit, theme, or concept, review the chart. Add any new understandings under the L—*What I Learned* column.
9. Have students generate a list of things they would still like to know. Add these under the L—*What I Learned* column.

Strategy in Action

The KWL chart is at home in any content area classroom. Topics to use can include the solar system (appropriate at all grade levels as part of a science unit), a book or novel (anything from a primary board book to a complex novel), the Pythagorean theorem or shapes (for math), the electoral college or Westward Expansion (for social studies).

Sharing and Reflection

- ❏ With a colleague, select a new concept in a content area that you will both teach. Use the KWL strategy in both of your classes. Tape your lessons and listen to, or view, them together, discussing how the use of the strategy affected students' comprehension, noting interesting responses.
- ❏ Think about ways in which you could use the KWL as an assessment tool. What did you learn about your students when the chart was started? Were there any surprises? Did your students have any misconceptions about the topic? How could students use this chart for self-assessment?

Tips and Hints

- ❏ A variation of the KWL strategy is KWHL. The addition of the H—*How Am I Going to Learn* column encourages students to think about resources and strategies they can use to find answers to their questions. First try the regular KWL strategy, then the variation, each time using material in the same subject area. Is there any difference in the way students gathered information or the level of comprehension? Which method of gathering information do you prefer? Why?

❏ Use the KWL as a preparatory activity when students are about to read, listen to, or view new informational material. After students have studied the material and the chart has been completed, ask students whether using the chart helped them remember information.

12

LIST-GROUP-LABEL

STRATEGY-AT-A-GLANCE

STRATEGY OVERVIEW
List-Group-Label is a strategy for thinking about and relating essential concepts that are part of a unit of study. It is most often used as a prereading activity to stimulate thinking and prepare students for assimilating information. It can also be used as a prewriting activity. As students look for relationships among the concepts, they reveal what they know (and don't know) about the concepts and the overall topic. Such information is helpful in identifying their backgrounds of experience and instructional needs.

INSTRUCTIONAL BENEFITS
- ❑ activates students' prior knowledge and sets purposes for learning
- ❑ encourages students to use new vocabulary that's related to the topic
- ❑ stimulates higher-order thinking
- ❑ helps the teacher assess the quantity and quality of students' prior knowledge

BEFORE, DURING, AFTER . . . ANYTIME
- ❑ before reading to prepare students to assimilate new information, then after reading for revision and closure
- ❑ before writing to stimulate thinking and review vocabulary
- ❑ anytime when reviewing previously learned information

Strategy Step-by-Step

1. For the topic or concept that's the focus of an upcoming lesson or unit, identify the essential vocabulary and put the words on a "list" in random

order. Try to keep the list to no more than twenty-five to thirty words—dealing with too many words at one time can be overwhelming. Make sure the words can be organized into categories.

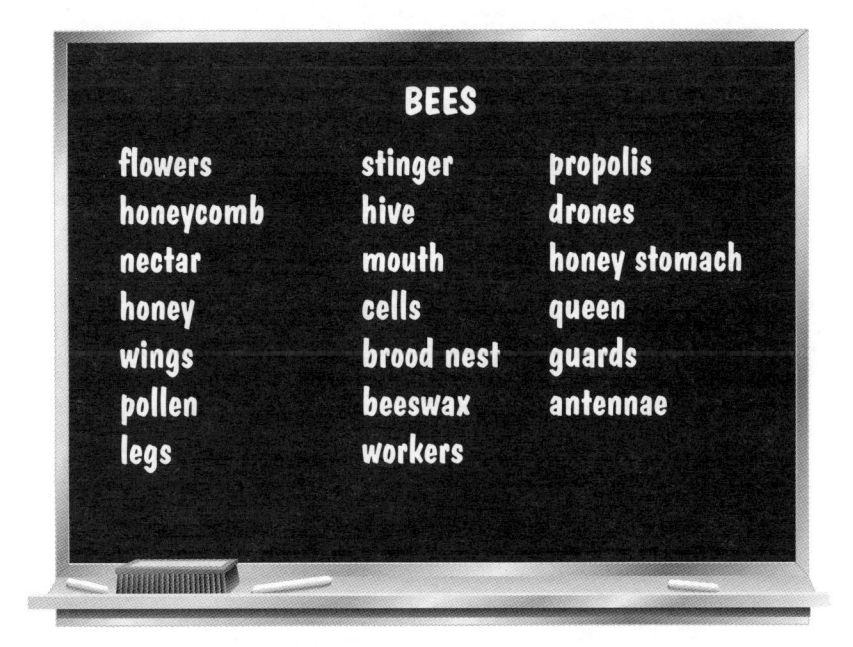

BEES

flowers	stinger	propolis
honeycomb	hive	drones
nectar	mouth	honey stomach
honey	cells	queen
wings	brood nest	guards
pollen	beeswax	antennae
legs	workers	

2. Announce the main topic, give students the list, and tell them that the words are important terms that have to do with the topic. Have students practice pronouncing the words.

3. Have students "group" the words into categories in terms of how they are related to the main topic. Students can work individually or in small groups. Tell them they should include each word on the list in a group and that if they aren't sure where to put any words they should make their best attempt and consider it a hypothesis. Students using the words shown on the blackboard above can form the group shown on the notebook on the following page.

wings
legs
stinger
mouth
propolis
honey stomach

4. Next, have students "label" the categories they created and give each category a title or explain how all the words in that group are related. For example, the group above might be labeled like this:

    Parts of a Bee

    wings

    legs

    stinger

    mouth

    propolis

    honey stomach

5. When students have finished grouping and labeling, have them share their hypotheses, then turn to the material to get more information. After reading, listening, or viewing, students should revise their original categories and labels to reflect what they learned from the material. In the example above, for instance, students would omit "propolis" from the category because they would learn that propolis is a kind of glue that bees use to repair a hive.

Strategy in Action

A variation of the List-Group-Label strategy is to present a topic to students and have them brainstorm a list of as many words as they can think of that are important words relating to the topic. Put the words on the board or on an overhead transparency. You may also want to show pictures of the topic as stimuli for this brainstorming. Then have students work in small groups, or individually, to group the words and label them as described above. Students can read, listen to, or view materials to get more information and then revise and add to their categories and labels as needed.

❏ Use List-Group-Label as a preparatory activity when students are about to read, listen to, or view some informational material. After students have studied the material and revised their lists, have them talk about the effects the strategy had on their ability to understand and remember the material.

❏ First try the regular List-Group-Label strategy, then the variation, each time using material in the same subject area. Is there any difference in students' response between the variations in the strategy? Which one do you prefer? Why?

❏ Use List-Group-Label to introduce lessons in two or three different subject areas. Do students respond about the same in each lesson or do you notice differences across content areas? If there are differences, how do you account for them?

Sharing and Reflection

❏ With a colleague, plan a List-Group-Label activity that you both use in your own classes. Tape your lessons and listen to or view them together, discussing how students handled the activity and noting interesting responses. Then invite a few other colleagues to learn about what you did and try the same activity with their students.

❏ Demonstrate List-Group-Label to your colleagues with material from an informational magazine article or the chapter of a book. Have them discuss their reactions as "students." Encourage them to try the strategy in their classrooms. Then meet again to compare notes and deepen your understanding of the strategy.

RATNER MEDIA AND TECHNOLOGY CENTER
JEWISH EDUCATION CENTER OF CLEVELAND

13

NOTETAKING

STRATEGY-AT-A-GLANCE

STRATEGY OVERVIEW
Notetaking while reading, listening, or viewing is a strategy for recording and organizing information in order to understand and remember it. As such, it's a way of using writing as a tool for learning. There are different strategies for notetaking, but regardless of the type used, a key to successful notetaking is regular review and revision of notes, which is emphasized here.

INSTRUCTIONAL BENEFITS
- ❑ enhances students' comprehension of instructional material
- ❑ helps students use their notes as learning/study aids
- ❑ shows students how to use notetaking independently

BEFORE, DURING, AFTER . . . ANYTIME
- ❑ any time you want students to keep track of and remember information. For example, when students are reading or doing hands-on activities
- ❑ anytime to help students improve their independent study skills

Strategy Step-by-Step

1. Model two or three processes of notetaking, and have students discuss which ones appeal to them most and why. (Students with different learning styles may prefer different types of notes.) Following are three different types of notes:

Double-Entry Notes

Students draw a vertical line down the center of the page. On the left they record key pieces of information from the learning material or experience; on the right, they restate or summarize the information and add sketches or comments to help them remember it.

Notes as Graphics

Students keep their notes in the form of graphic organizers, arranging the ideas on the page in ways that make the relationships clear. (See "Graphic Organizers," pages 20–23, for more explanation.) Some students like to use different colors in their graphic-organizer notes—red for causes and effects, blue for important dates, green for important names, etc.

Main Idea/Detail Notes

Students draw a horizontal line near the top of the page. Above it they write a main idea from the material. Below it they write details that support that main idea. Students may decide to put two or three main idea/detail arrangements on a page, enclosing each one in a box to set it apart from the others.

1. Have students try the different notetaking strategies so they become familiar with them and are beginning to use them regularly. Encourage them to shift from one type of strategy to another, depending on the kinds of material with which they are working.

2. Have students focus on taking especially careful notes in one subject area for a week or two. At the end of the time, have students bring all their notes to class and do one or more of the following activities designed to help students make active use of their notes. Model as needed to show them what to do.

Student Guidelines

- With a partner, engage in the Read-Talk-Write strategy with your notes as the reading material. That is, read your notes individually, put them aside, take turns talking about what you learned, then write what you understand about the topic on new paper. Compare what you write with your original notes to see if you remembered all the important points. (See "Read-Talk-Write," pages 58–61, for more explanation.)
- Study a page of graphic-organizer notes, cover it up, and do your best to reproduce it from memory. Then check the original to see how much you remembered.
- Review your notes for a week, then revise them so that the week's study is represented on only one page. That means condensing to retain only the most important points, combining graphics as possible, etc. (If students do this successively through a unit of study, they will benefit greatly from the reviewing and rethinking they'll do as they repeatedly condense to one page. They keep all the original notes for reference as well as the one-page summaries.)

Strategy in Action

- Before giving students any instruction in notetaking, have them take notes while reading the first half of a chapter from a science or social studies book. Then, model one or more of the notetaking strategies described above and have students use one when they read the rest of the chapter. Have students compare their notes from the two occasions and discuss how the instruction has affected their notetaking behavior.
- Have students take notes regularly for several weeks or more, revising their notes down to one page at the end of each week.
- Have students take notes individually on a lesson or unit, then meet in groups to compare their notes and create a new set of notes—as a group—that reflects all their understandings. What effect does the collaborative review and notetaking have on students' understanding?

Sharing and Reflection

❏ Have students try different notetaking strategies and share examples of what they consider good sets of notes. With their permission, share their examples with your colleagues and tell them what you've been doing in your classroom to improve students' notetaking skills.

❏ Invite your colleagues to focus on notetaking in their classes for at least a month, model notetaking strategies, and do some of the activities described above. Meet at the end of the time to discuss any differences you notice in students' comprehension and retention.

❏ Note any of the following in your teacher journal. Do you notice any difference in the students' grasp of the material? in their retention of important ideas? in the quality of their notes as they undertake notetaking?

POSSIBLE SENTENCES

STRATEGY-AT-A-GLANCE

STRATEGY OVERVIEW
Possible sentences is a prereading strategy that is appropriate for either narrative or expository material. Students are given several words from the material and are asked to create one or more sentences with them. Then they read to find out how the words are actually used by the author.

INSTRUCTIONAL BENEFITS
- activates prior knowledge before reading
- encourages students to read with purpose and interest
- enhances comprehension of the material
- keeps students actively involved before, during, and after reading

BEFORE, DURING, AFTER . . . ANYTIME
- before reading a short story or a chapter in a novel
- before reading expository material such as an article or textbook chapter

Strategy Step-by-Step

1. Select several important words from the material that could be used in different ways in one or more sentences. You'll probably want to choose five or six words at a minimum. Increase the number if students are familiar with the strategy and you want to give them a greater challenge. Tell students that all the words come from material they are about to read and that you want them to create one or more sentences to show how they think the words might be used.

2. Explain that you'll be interested in different responses even if they seem odd. Remind them that the activity is called "Possible Sentences" because there are several possible ways the words could be used in sentences, including the student responses.

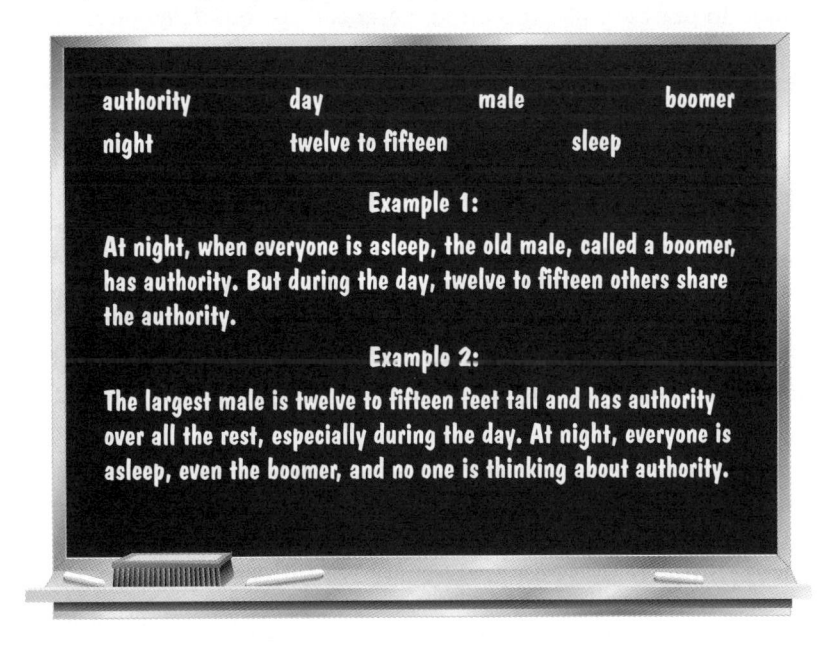

> authority   day   male   boomer
> night   twelve to fifteen   sleep
>
> **Example 1:**
> At night, when everyone is asleep, the old male, called a boomer, has authority. But during the day, twelve to fifteen others share the authority.
>
> **Example 2:**
> The largest male is twelve to fifteen feet tall and has authority over all the rest, especially during the day. At night, everyone is asleep, even the boomer, and no one is thinking about authority.

3. Have students share their sentences and discuss what they think they'll be reading about. Then have them read the material and compare the way the author uses the words with the way they used them in their own sentences.

   Students are usually very interested in reading at this point because they're curious about how the words are actually used. Their interest and attention enhance their comprehension. On the following page is part of the selection from which the words were taken for the example above. The full selection gives more information about kangaroos.

Kangaroos

Kangaroos live in groups, called "mobs." A mob's leader is the largest male—an old boomer who has proved his dominance and who fights other males when they challenge his authority. The boss kangaroo leads the mob to places where food and water can be found. When they travel, kangaroos can move very fast indeed. Under ordinary conditions, they run twelve to fifteen miles an hour, but they can run twice as fast if they are in a hurry.

Strategy in Action

❑ Use possible sentences to introduce the reading of social studies, health, or science materials. If students are not familiar with the strategy, use some words that are key concepts that may be unfamiliar to students and others that are simple, familiar words. Notice how the students respond. In what way do you think their comprehension was affected by the use of the strategy?

❑ Use possible sentences to introduce the reading of a work of literature such as a short story. Try including one or two character names along with key words that relate to the setting and plot. How do you think students' interest and comprehension was affected by using the strategy?

Reflections and Review

❑ Work with a colleague to select words for possible sentences from material that you both can use with your classes. After you have each conducted your lessons, compare notes on how your students responded to the activity.

❑ Use possible sentences several times until you are familiar with it. Save examples of your students' sentences and jot down anecdotes from your lessons that illustrate what you think were especially good moments of discussion. Share what you have learned with your colleagues.

❑ Try using possible sentences repeatedly during a unit of instruction, each time using one or two words from the previous array. What effect do you think this had on the connections students were able to make from one part of the unit to the next?

Tips and Hints

Some teachers prefer telling their students the topic when they present the words for possible sentences, having noticed that students can usually create sentences more easily if they have the topic as a guide. This is certainly a reasonable alternative to presenting the words alone. Try both ways and see which one you like the best.

15

READ-TALK-WRITE

STRATEGY-AT-A-GLANCE

STRATEGY OVERVIEW
This strategy helps students read carefully and put the information they've read in their own words. Students read individually, then pair up and take turns telling their partners what they read—without looking at the text. After students have talked, they write what they learned. Because students talk first and then write, the writing is in their own words rather than copied from the text. Students can use this strategy on their own when they study, take notes for research papers, or want to improve their comprehension of almost any informational material.

INSTRUCTIONAL BENEFITS
❏ helps students learn to paraphrase information
❏ encourages students to monitor their comprehension while reading
❏ cements learning by having students restate ideas orally and in writing
❏ builds listening and speaking skills
❏ gives meaningful practice with writing

BEFORE, DURING, AFTER . . . ANYTIME
❏ any time students need extra help with comprehension
❏ any time students are doing research for written reports
❏ anytime when teaching students independent study skills

Strategy Step-by-Step

Have the whole class go through the steps together several times until they understand what to do. Continue to use the strategy with the whole class periodically, and have students use it with a partner when they're studying or taking notes for reports.

1. **Read**

    Students all read silently for a set period of time. Take just a few minutes for the reading when they're first learning the strategy; increase the time as they gain experience. Everyone can read the same material, or each person can be reading something different. When time is up, have students close their books.

2. **Talk**

    Pair students up and designate one member of the pair "A" and the other "B." Have all the A members of the pair (or all the B members) talk to their partners simultaneously, telling as much as they can remember from their reading without looking back at the text. Have them all start and stop when you give the signal.

    Next, the other partners talk, again telling as much as they can remember from reading. They may repeat what their partners said if they can't think of anything else to say, but they should try to state the repeated ideas in different words. Again, start and stop them with signals.

    Talkers must do their best to talk nonstop, repeating what they said if they can't think of any new ideas. Listeners must listen attentively but may not say anything until it's their turn to talk.

3. **Write**

    Each student now writes what he or she learned from reading (as well as talking and listening), still keeping books closed. When students have written as much as they can, they can reread the text to check details if they wish.

Strategy in Action

- ❏ First, have students read a section from a content-area text and write what they learned, referring to the text if they wish. Then, show them how to do Read-Talk-Write and have them use it with a different section of the same book. Ask students to compare their comprehension and writing under the two different conditions and discuss in what ways Read-Talk-Write affected their responses.

❏ Assign a one-page research report to students and collect the papers. Then show them how to use Read-Talk-Write and have them use it to do a second report (on the same topic or on another topic). Compare the reports. Is the second one better in terms of the ideas being written in the students' own words?

Review and Reflection

❏ Tell your colleagues about your use of Read-Talk-Write with your students. Show them examples of the students' work, especially those papers that illustrate clear understanding of concepts expressed in the students' own words.
❏ Work with another teacher to plan a Read-Talk-Write lesson that you can both use. After you've each taught the lesson to your own classes, compare notes. Then share your experiences and reflections with other colleagues.

Tips and Hints

❏ To start, model the process of reading and putting ideas in your own words orally, working with a text that you and the students have previously read together silently. Hearing you put the ideas into your own words will help students understand how to break away from the original wording.
❏ Model the process of writing after talking so that students can see how to go from oral paraphrasing to putting the ideas in writing.
❏ Have students use this strategy regularly in class with content-area text materials to help them improve their comprehension.
❏ Tell students that it's important to verbalize what they've read and to say things in their own words. It's less important to remember everything they read since they can always go back and reread.
❏ When the whole class is working with the same text, have several students read their writings aloud at the end of the activity so that students can hear different ways the ideas can be put in writing.

❏ Have students work in Read-Talk-Write pairs when they're doing research for reports. It's fine for them to talk or listen to each other when they're reading different materials.

16

READERS' THEATER

STRATEGY-AT-A-GLANCE

STRATEGY OVERVIEW
Readers' theater involves students reading a play aloud that they have created themselves based on a narrative work or a segment from a book. The term is also used to refer to reading aloud plays that have been written especially for use by students. In either case, students work collaboratively on their reading, practicing their parts together, and then reading to an audience.

INSTRUCTIONAL BENEFITS
- ❏ develops oral reading and oral expression skills
- ❏ deepens comprehension of a narrative text
- ❏ integrates reading, writing, listening, and speaking
- ❏ compares and contrasts narration and drama

BEFORE, DURING, AFTER . . . ANYTIME
- ❏ as a follow-up to reading a narrative work of literature
- ❏ anytime when teaching drama as a form of literature

Strategy Step-by-Step

To create a play with students, choose a narrative work students are familiar with and that lends itself to dramatization. Try starting with a simply structured folk tale and have students go through the process with you step by step, contributing ideas as you lead the way.

1. Reread the story to decide where to break it into acts. Lead students to see why some places make better breaking points than others because they involve major turning points in the story.

2. Within each act, reread again to review the action and discuss which characters are involved. Also decide how the narrator will make transitions between scenes. (Some readers' theater plays do not need narrators, but narrators are useful for handling transitions and giving other information that would be difficult to convey with dialogue alone.)

3. Decide on the sequence of events and dialogue within each act. Using the story text as a guide, write the dialogue, the narrator's statements, and directions to the readers. In working with you on this, students should see that descriptions and information given in stories often need to be worked in to the dialogue. For example, here's part of the text of a folk tale (retold here for illustration), and a play script that was written from it.

The Bremen Town Musicians

Once upon a time, a donkey grew so old and tired that his master decided it was time to get rid of him. The donkey sensed this and before the master could lead him to slaughter, he ran away, following the road to Bremen. As he trotted along, he thought to himself that once he got to town he would look for work as a musician.

Before long he came upon a hound who was lying, exhausted, by the side of the road. "What's wrong, my friend?" asked the donkey.

"Poor me!" said the dog. "Because I can no longer hunt, my master was going to have me put to sleep. I saved my life by running away, but what will I do now?"

—Jacob Grimm 1998

The Bremen Town Musicians: A Play

Narrator: After many years of carrying heavy loads, a donkey overheard his master saying it was time to get rid of him. So he ran away. As our story opens, the donkey is on the road to Bremen, a town far from his master's farm.

Donkey: Hee-haw! Hee-haw! I can't believe my master was going to send me to the slaughter house! It's a good thing I escaped. I don't know what

I'll do when I get to Bremen, but I think I'd like to try being a musician. Anything but carrying heavy loads on my back! (Pause) Oh my! That dog up ahead looks like he's in trouble!

Dog: Ohhhh! Ohhhh!

Donkey: Hello there, Dog. You sound very upset. What's the matter?

Dog: I served my master faithfully for many years, but when I grew too old to hunt with him, he told his wife he was going to have me put to sleep. I saved my life by running away, but what will I do now?

Continue working back and forth between the narrative and the developing play script until you and your students have completed a first draft.

4. Have students take roles and read the draft aloud to see how it sounds and to see if the important points of the story are all included. Revise as needed.
5. Prepare a final version and make copies for students. Have them practice reading the play aloud several times until they're ready to perform it for an audience.

You may want to create several readers' theater plays with students before having them try one on their own. When you think they're ready, have them work in small groups to turn a story into a play, then read it aloud to the rest of the class.

Strategy in Action

Fictional and true historical accounts of the Revolutionary and Civil Wars, the women's suffrage and civil rights movements, and current newspaper and magazine articles are among the many sources that can be used in a social studies class for employing the readers' theater strategy.

Sharing and Reflection

Use readers' theater at the same time a colleague is using it in his or her class. Compare notes, exchange ideas, and discuss what you're observing and learning. Have the students read their plays to the other class or exchange scripts for reading aloud.

❏ As students are working in groups on their own readers' theater plays, circulate and listen in on the conversations. What kinds of comprehension and thinking skills do you notice being used? Jot down some examples of how this activity requires deeper comprehension than usual and share your findings with colleagues.

Tips and Hints

❏ As a first step, create your own readers' theater script from a story you and the class have enjoyed. If possible, include some lines for a "chorus" that all students can read together so that the whole class can be involved. Have students read the play several times until they are reading smoothly and confidently. (You may want to use a prepared script for this activity instead of creating your own.)

❏ Have students work in small groups to create plays from familiar folk tales. When they've prepared their scripts, have groups exchange them and read each other's plays aloud.

❏ Have different groups of students create plays from the same story that all have read and discussed in class. Have each group read aloud its play, assigning parts to others as needed. Then have the class discuss the similarities among and differences between the scripts.

17

RESTATING/ PARAPHRASING

STRATEGY-AT-A-GLANCE

STRATEGY OVERVIEW
Restating or paraphrasing involves putting material that someone else has said or written into your own words. This form of speaking or writing is both a tool for learning and a means of monitoring or checking comprehension.

INSTRUCTIONAL BENEFITS
- ❏ develops comprehension
- ❏ checks comprehension
- ❏ helps students monitor their own comprehension
- ❏ helps students incorporate material into their written work without copying it word for word

BEFORE, DURING, AFTER . . . ANYTIME
- ❏ after reading, listening, or viewing to develop comprehension
- ❏ anytime to check comprehension
- ❏ during research-report units when students are working source material into their papers

Strategy Step-by-Step

Students learn to restate and paraphrase information by observing others do it and by being asked to do it themselves regularly. The following process can help.

1. Have students read with you a paragraph from an expository text. Then, paraphrase each sentence in writing as they watch.

2. Write the new sentences on the board or use an overhead projector so that students can see the differences between the original and your paraphrased version.
3. Have students do the paraphrasing of another paragraph with you. Take a sentence or two at a time, and record their restatements on the board.
4. Help students revise if they have trouble breaking away from the vocabulary and syntax of the original. When finished, read aloud the original and then the new paragraph to emphasize the differences.
5. After you've modeled paraphrasing, have students work in small groups to paraphrase short pieces of expository text, e.g., a paragraph or two from a content-area textbook. Have groups share their work and discuss which paraphrased statements are especially good because the vocabulary and sentence structure is notably different from the original.

Strategy in Action

❏ Like most teachers, you probably paraphrase your own words frequently when you're explaining things. If you call attention to this modeling, you'll help students understand how to do it on their own. Here's an example:

The main food of bees is nectar that they collect from flowers. Here's another way to say that—a way to paraphrase it: Bees go from flower to flower gathering sweet juice called nectar, and that nectar is the main thing they eat.

❏ In discussions, ask students to restate instructional material and your own explanations regularly by saying "What does that actually mean? Say it in your own words." If students can't explain something in their own words, chances are they don't understand it very well, so whenever you encourage them to paraphrase in this way, you give yourself a chance to monitor their comprehension.

❏ Teach students to read, close the book, and restate the ideas in their own words when they are studying. This useful technique is one step in such tried-and-true study methods as SQ3R (Survey, Question, Read, Recite, Review) and PQRST (Preview, Question, Read, Summarize, Test). Encourage students to monitor their comprehension when they're reading by pausing in this way to see if they can explain what they're reading.

❏ When students are taking notes in preparation for writing a research report, have them work in pairs to use the Read-Talk-Write strategy (see "Read-Talk-Write," pages 58–61). This can help them think about what they've read and state it in their own words before they write it in their notes.

Sharing and Reflection

❏ Work with one or more colleagues to emphasize restating and paraphrasing in your classes. Get together regularly to share the activities you're using and to talk about what effect your emphasis is having on students' comprehension.

❏ Do the first classroom activity described above, and find several good examples of students who improved their writing from the first to the second report. Share these with colleagues and explain how you handled the two assignments. Encourage them to try the activity themselves and get back together to discuss the results.

❏ Focus on restating and paraphrasing for a full week. Whenever you're discussing a reading assignment or explaining something to students, stop periodically to have them restate the information in their own words. Or have students write their restatements in their learning logs. What effect does this have on students' attention and comprehension? Do they improve their ability to restate information by the end of the week?

Tips and Hints

Before you've taught students to paraphrase, assign them a one-page research report that requires getting information from a book, periodical, Web site, or encyclopedia. Collect the papers and put them aside. Then teach students to paraphrase (as described above) and have them do the report assignment again. Compare the two sets of papers and have students compare them as well. Do you see improvement in the extent to which the information is in the students' own words? Do the students see the difference?

18

SATURATION REPORTING

STRATEGY-AT-A-GLANCE

STRATEGY OVERVIEW
A saturation report is an original piece of reporting that's based on the student's observations of an occasion or a place. To write such an eye-witness report, students "saturate" themselves with sights and sounds, taking notes on the spot, then write an account that makes the place or occasion come alive for readers while it conveys the writer's general impression of the experience.

INSTRUCTIONAL BENEFITS
- ❏ stimulates interesting, original expository writing
- ❏ develops observation and reporting skills
- ❏ connects the writing process directly to students' own lives and experiences
- ❏ refines and extends general writing abilities
- ❏ prepares students for writing other kinds of reports, for example, I-Search reports and research reports

BEFORE, DURING, AFTER . . . ANYTIME
- ❏ anytime as a language arts writing assignment
- ❏ anytime as a writing assignment in content areas (having students report on a place or occasion that relates to the unit of study)
- ❏ before having students complete reports based on researching information in texts

Strategy Step-by-Step

You will probably want to give students several days or more to complete the following sequence.

18

1. Decide on the places or occasions in school or in the community that you want to assign for saturation reports, or have students brainstorm ideas with you. Suggestions are listed below. In-school assignments are suitable for almost all students but are especially good for younger students; older students might go farther afield (with parental permission).

In the School	**Outside the School**
cafeteria	hospital emergency room
library/media center	grocery store or other retail store
lobby or main office	public library reading room
playground	restaurant or snack bar
main hallway	museum or public park
whole-school assembly	parade or other celebration
school sports event	public sports event
science fair	live concert

2. Assign a place or occasion to each student or to pairs. (Several can be given the same assignment.) Hand out directions and send students out to do their assignment.

DIRECTIONS

Name _____ Assignment _____

You've been given a plum assignment, Reporter! At your assignment, observe quietly and carefully, and "saturate" yourself with details and impressions for your report.

Don't forget to take notes! Write down interesting sights, sounds, and smells. Notice what people are wearing, doing, and saying. Notice details of the surroundings.

Jot down words and phrases, and draw sketches. Take it all in! Think about the overall impression you get from the place that you will convey in your report.

3. Back in class, have students look over their notes and decide on the general impression they got from their place or occasion. For instance, a school cafeteria might present a picture of noisy exuberance and camaraderie, while a public library reading room might have an atmosphere of studious concentration. Think of the general impression as the focus of the report—the main idea that all the details will support.

4. When students are ready to write their first drafts, stress the importance of telling details and vivid descriptive words. The following kinds of modeling will help students plan and write their first drafts:
   - **From you** Write a paragraph or two on a transparency while students watch.
   - **From other students** Let students read good examples of saturation reports from other classes.
   - **From professional writers** Have students read eye-witness reports in magazines and newspapers to see how professional writers convey their impressions of places and events.

5. Have students write first drafts, then meet in small groups to help each other sharpen the focus, choose better words, rearrange details for maximum effect, and in other ways revise their drafts.

6. Publish the saturation reports. For instance, collect them in a notebook for display in the school media center; circulate them to other classes; post them in the hall or on the school or district's Web site. Keep copies to use as examples for the next round of reports and for next year's students.

Strategy in Action

Beyond the language arts classroom, Saturation Reports can be used in social studies classes where students can be asked to report on a historical place that they visit on a field trip.

Sharing and Reflection

❏ Have students write traditional reports individually (based on information they get from reading) and then do individual saturation reports. What differences do you see between the two sets of papers? If your students are like most, their saturation reports will be written in their own, natural language rather than sounding like they've been copied from reference materials.

❏ Plan to have students do four or five saturation reports during the school year. (They can return to the same places or go to new ones.) Keep the reports, each time comparing the latest with the earlier ones. Do the reports improve? In what ways? What other differences do you notice from one occasion to the next?

❏ Tell a group of interested colleagues how you've been using saturation reports, showing examples of your students' work to illustrate. What advantages of this kind of writing do you emphasize with your colleagues?

❏ Collaborate with another teacher on having your classes do saturation reports that they share with each other. Meet with the other teacher regularly to plan activities and discuss your observations about the strategy.

Tips and Hints

Assign pairs of students places or occasions and have them work together to observe, take notes, draft, and revise. Compare the finished reports with other writing students have done individually. Two-person reports are especially suitable for students who are less experienced writers, and because collaboration is usually enjoyable, students may tend to write more and write better.

19

STORYTELLING

STRATEGY-AT-A-GLANCE

STRATEGY OVERVIEW
Storytelling involves a teacher presenting a story orally without using the book or notes. It is an activity with a long tradition—from pre-literate cultures, where stories preserved important historical and cultural information and values, to present-day society where—in livings rooms and classrooms and at festivals—stories are used for entertainment and cultural transmission.

INSTRUCTIONAL BENEFITS
- ❏ fosters listening comprehension and sense of story
- ❏ builds listening vocabulary and concepts
- ❏ develops and refines general oral language abilities
- ❏ improves attention skills
- ❏ develops appreciation for literature
- ❏ stimulates verbal and nonverbal response to literature

BEFORE, DURING, AFTER . . . ANYTIME
- ❏ anytime as a regular language arts/literature activity
- ❏ anytime in the content areas to enliven the study of people and events

Strategy Step-by-Step

1. Choose a story that you already know fairly well and that you think your students would enjoy. Stories from the oral tradition of various cultures are ideal for telling, such as folk tales, fairy tales, and myths. Examples of such stories that are well received at various grade levels include:

The Mitten (Brett 1996): Animals of increasing size crawl into a mitten to keep warm until, with one too many, the mitten pops.

Hansel and Gretel (Stevenson 1999): Two children use their ingenuity to escape from a witch and find their way home.

The Algonquin Cinderella (Shah 1979): An interesting version of the classic theme of achieving good fortune after a struggle.

2. Create an outline or graphic (or other written notes) of the main characters and events of the tale to help you learn the story. Study your notes, referring to the story text as needed, until you know the sequence of events by heart. Compose strong first and last sentences and learn them by heart.

3. Practice telling the story often until you feel you know it thoroughly. Don't try to memorize it; just learn it well. Practice in private at first, then rehearse with people who make you feel comfortable trying something new. Refer to your notes less and less until you don't need them at all.

4. Tell the story to your class. Introduce the event with a simple signal that you can then make a pleasant storytelling ritual, for instance, ring a small bell. Follow up the story with one or more activities with students that elicit creative response. Following are examples of such activities:

   - **Dramatizing.** Do this impromptu acting out of the story with minimal props several times after a story, allowing different students to express their interpretations of the tale.
   - **Drawing.** Have students draw the scene that's the most meaningful or important to them, then share their drawings and talk about why they chose to draw those scenes.
   - **Writing.** Have students write in response to the story, telling which part they liked best and why, what they think of the various characters, and what the story means to them.
   - **Discussing.** Invite personal response to the story by asking one or more open-ended questions such as:

     What was the most important part of the story to you? Why was that part especially important to you?

     Which character do you sympathize with the most? The least? Why?

Was the ending satisfying to you? Why? If not, how do you think the story should end?

How do you visualize the various characters? The settings? Which scene can you picture most vividly?

Is this story like any other story you know? In what way are the stories similar? Different?

5. When students enjoy a story, tell it several times over the course of a week or two. Repeated telling enhances comprehension and provides opportunities for deeper reflection on the story's meaning.

Strategy in Action

Myths and folk tales surrounding natural occurrences (Thor's drum making thunder) can be used as a springboard in science to promote study of the actual phenomenon (weather fronts). Use narratives and stories from cultures not dominant in your school in social studies class.

Sharing and Reflection

❑ Team up with a colleague who's also interested in storytelling. Select different stories to learn, and tell them to both classes. Compare notes on the students' responses during the tellings and follow-up activities.

❑ Start a storytelling club among interested colleagues. Share stories and follow-up activities with each other, tell stories in each other's classes, and share observations about how you make this strategy work for you.

❑ Tell several different kinds of stories to your students to observe how they respond to each one. For instance, use some with mostly entertainment value as well as some with more serious themes that lead to reflection on their meanings. Do you notice any difference in students' attention and response?

❑ Establish a regular time for storytelling and set it off clearly from other activities with a story time signal at the start and finish. Over time, do you notice any difference in students' attention and interest during this time?

Tips and Hints

Keep a story notebook with story texts and story maps of those you've used along with notes on the follow-up activities you've tried and comments on your students' responses. Such a notebook can become an excellent resource from one year to the next as you build your storytelling repertoire.

20

STRIP STORY

STRATEGY-AT-A-GLANCE

STRATEGY OVERVIEW
A strip story is one or more paragraphs that have been rewritten as a list of sentences in mixed-up order. Students cut out the sentences and put them in the right order. The strategy can be used with both narrative and expository texts.

INSTRUCTIONAL BENEFITS
- builds comprehension skills by developing understanding of how statements in a text are related
- gives students practice in thinking logically about a text
- develops students' writing abilities by giving them a chance to think like writers

BEFORE, DURING, AFTER . . . ANYTIME
- anytime as a teacher-directed comprehension activity
- anytime as a small-group/individual comprehension practice activity

Strategy Step-by-Step

1. Model the process first with a short paragraph. Print or type each sentence on a strip of paper or overhead transparency, and then arrange them in a mixed-up order.

Bees and Flowers

They make honey from the nectar and use it and pollen as food.

When the bees gather pollen, they spread it on different flowers.

Flowers provide food for bees.

This spreading, called pollination, helps the plants reproduce.

Many plants depend on bees for the pollination they need.

Bees collect pollen and nectar from the flowers they visit.

2. Present the mixed-up sentences to the class and rearrange them while they watch, explaining your thinking as you go. For instance, you'll want to call attention to transition words such as "next" or "then" or pronouns that refer to nouns—all of which are clues to sentence order. You may want to continue to demonstrate as above with two or three other paragraphs to make sure students understand how to think about strip stories. To continue the example, following is the original order of the sentences shown above along with reasoning that might be shared with students:

Bees and Flowers

Flowers provide food for bees.

Bees collect pollen and nectar from the flowers they visit.

They make honey from the nectar and use it and pollen as food.

When the bees gather pollen, they spread it on different flowers.

This spreading, called pollination, helps the plants reproduce.

Many plants depend on bees for the pollination they need.

Reasons to support the above arrangement:

- The first sentence is a general statement about how flowers help bees. It's developed further in the following two sentences, so it belongs before them.
- What's described in the second sentence happens first, and what's described in the third sentence happens next.
- Now the paragraph shifts to tell about how bees help flowers. First, the bees spread pollen as they gather it.
- "This spreading" in the next sentence is a clue that the sentence comes after the first reference to spreading.
- The last sentence explains how important the bees' actions are to the plants. A clue to this sentence's position is the word "pollination." The word was defined in an earlier sentence, so it makes sense that this sentence comes after that one.

3. Next, have students work in small groups to rearrange a new set of sentences from a paragraph that's well structured and fairly easy to re-create. Have groups compare their arrangements and discuss their reasons for positioning the sentences as they did. Some sets of strips can be arranged in more than one way, so what's most important here is the reasoning behind the arrangement, not the arrangement itself. As students become familiar with the process, gradually introduce longer and more challenging strip stories.

Because strip stories are like puzzles, most students enjoy doing them. With frequent practice, they can refine and extend their comprehension skills significantly. That's because they're focusing not just on individual words and sentences but on the relationships among ideas and the overall meaning of the paragraphs.

Strategy in Action

- ❏ As a prereading activity, give students sentence strips made from the first paragraph of a story they haven't read before. What effect do you think the activity had on students' interest in reading the rest of the story?

- ❏ Have students do one or more strip stories for both narrative and expository texts. Have them talk about which paragraphs were easiest to re-create and why. Some students may find narrative texts easier; others may prefer exposition. Being aware of these differences can help you and the students recognize their unique strengths and weaknesses with text comprehension.

- ❏ When students are familiar with this strategy, invite them to make up their own strip stories to exchange with one another or to put in a classroom Strip Story Center. Have students print or type the sentences clearly on strips of the same size and put the strips in a envelope (with the topic printed on the outside). Have them put the solution (the original paragraph) in the envelope, too, or collect the solutions and keep them in one answer keys folder.

Sharing and Reflection

- ❏ Collaborate with a colleague to prepare strip stories that you both can use. Choose paragraphs from a variety of materials and discuss with each other which ones were easiest and why and how your students fared overall.
- ❏ Have students work in small groups to do different strip stories every day for a week or more. Notice if students handle the task more easily after this extended practice. Share your observations with your colleagues.

TEAM WEBBING

STRATEGY-AT-A-GLANCE

STRATEGY OVERVIEW
Team webbing is a cooperative-group writing activity in which each team starts a web of ideas and then moves from station to station around the room, adding their ideas to the webs that other groups started. When the teams return to the webs they started, they read the ideas that have been added, discuss their responses, and raise questions. This strategy incorporates reading, writing, speaking, and listening in a natural, fluid way.

INSTRUCTIONAL BENEFITS
- helps students think about what they know and write it in their own words
- cements learning by having students restate ideas orally and in writing
- encourages students to listen to and read each other's ideas
- encourages students to generate their own questions about things they've learned or are studying

BEFORE, DURING, AFTER . . . ANYTIME
- after a lesson or unit to review and restate the information
- before a lesson or unit to activate prior knowledge and set purposes for learning

Strategy Step-by-Step

This is a whole-class activity. Students may need to do it a few times before they can move smoothly and make good written contributions to the webs.

1. Organize the class into four or five teams and establish a home base for each team, which can simply be an area where desks are pushed to-

gether. Home bases should be positioned so that students can move easily from one to the other. There should also be enough space around each base for teams to gather and write. You may want to have students push their chairs under their desks and stand during the whole activity.

2. Give each team a large sheet of sturdy paper (at least twelve inches by eighteen inches) and ballpoint pens or pencils of the same color, for example, Team A gets red pens, Team B gets blue pens, Team C gets green pens, and so on. All members of a team will need a pen.

3. Have someone on each team write the topic in the center of the paper and draw a circle around it. You can give each team the same topic, or you can assign a different topic to each team, perhaps subtopics of a main topic you've been studying.

4. Have each team create a web of ideas around the topic by writing things that they know about the topic on lines that radiate from the circled topic. Have students write statements (sentences) rather than single words or phrases. All students should write at the same time and talk about what they're writing if they want to. Give the teams five minutes or more to write. Then stop everyone at once.

5. Have students take their pens with them and, staying in teams, move to the next station. Have teams move in the same direction (clockwise or counterclockwise) to keep the movement smooth. When they get to the next station, they should do the following:
    - Read what's already on the web at that station.
    - Add new ideas if they can. If they can't think of new ideas, they can write the same ideas in different words.
    - If they can't think of words to write, they can sketch what they're thinking. (This is a good alternative for students who do not yet write easily.)

6. Have students rotate through all the stations, reading and writing, until they return to their home base. At their home base, they should do the following:
    - Read all the ideas on the web they started.
    - Identify one or two statements they think are especially good or interesting and share them with the whole class.
    - Think of one or two questions they have about the items the other teams added to their web.

As students read and discuss the completed webs, discourage criticism about what "they" added to "our" web. Instead, encourage questions and suggestions for revising statements that other team members added. This time of reflection and discussion should be an occasion for students to refine and extend their comprehension of the material. Some classes may need guidance and practice to interact effectively.

Strategy in Action

- ❏ Use team webbing as an end-of-unit activity in any content area. When teams have completed their webs, have students write individual summaries of what they learned, using their team's web as a source of ideas. How well do the teams handle themselves when they are working on the webs? How well do students interact in the post-webbing discussion? How good are their summaries?

- ❏ Use team webbing as a follow-up to reading a novel or a biography. Assign a different character to each team as the topic of their web so that as teams rotate they write their ideas about a different character each time. How do you think the webbing affects their reflections? What kinds of questions do they raise? What can you have students do with the completed webs?

- ❏ Have students use the team-webbing strategy as a prereading activity in a content-area unit and then do it again (adding to the same webs) after completing the unit.

Sharing and Reflection

- ❏ Show your colleagues some of the webs your students created with the team-webbing strategy and explain how you directed the activity. Give any tips you've discovered that make the strategy work well for you.

- ❏ Use team webbing with your class at the same time another teacher uses it with his or her class. Compare notes on how well your students did, and discuss ideas for how you could make the next time even better. Then share your experiences and reflections with other colleagues.

22

THINK-PAIR-SHARE

STRATEGY-AT-A-GLANCE

STRATEGY OVERVIEW

Think-Pair-Share is a strategy for getting students to respond more frequently in class by interacting with each other as well as with the teacher. The teacher poses the question or gives a prompt. Students then follow these steps:

- ❏ Think (individually) about your response.
- ❏ Pair with another student and discuss your ideas.
- ❏ Share your thinking with the rest of the class.

The teacher allows a few minutes for each step, then moves students to the next step with a signal. Some teachers use hand signals, while others use a small bell or other audio signal. When students are experienced with the routine, they can do it on their own when they're working in small groups.

INSTRUCTIONAL BENEFITS

- ❏ increases time on task and active involvement
- ❏ provides time for students to formulate and "rehearse" their responses before offering them to the whole class
- ❏ gives students a chance to talk in order to learn
- ❏ encourages students to listen each other
- ❏ allows a change of pace from the usual interaction pattern, i.e., teacher talks, one student talks, teacher talks

BEFORE, DURING, AFTER . . . ANYTIME

- ❏ anytime when conducting whole-class discussions
- ❏ any time students discuss ideas in small groups

Strategy Step-by-Step

1. Explain the steps, making sure students understand the purpose of each step. As a reminder, you may want to post a brief explanation, an example of which follows:

   ### Think — Pair — Share

   Think means: concentrate on the question, think about possible responses, and decide what to say

   Pair means: discuss ideas with a partner before presenting them to the whole class

   Share means: tell your ideas to the whole class when it is your turn

2. Decide on the signal you'll use to indicate the start of each step. For instance, one ring of a small bell could mean Think; two rings could mean Pair; three rings could mean Time to Share. If you want to use hand signals, try two fingers touching the head for Think, crossed fingers or clasped hands for Pair, and a hand extended outward, palm up, for Share. Practice the signals with students until they are all familiar with them.

3. Practice Think-Pair-Share frequently, at least once every day, when you're conducting whole-class activities. Good times to use the strategy include:
   - when discussing a work of literature
   - when discussing an informational reading selection
   - during a hands-on science or math activity
   - when discussing a film or other visual presentation
   - during problem-solving activities
   - as a prewriting activity for generating ideas

Strategy in Action

❏ Before teaching students Think-Pair-Share, tape a whole-class discussion of a reading or listening selection. When you listen to the tape, make note of how many students respond and how long each responder talks. Then teach Think-Pair-Share, and after some practice, tape another whole-class discussion in which you use the strategy. Compare these responses with the ones in the other taped discussion. What do you notice?

❏ Focus on a few students who are ordinarily reluctant to speak out in class. How does Think-Pair-Share affect their willingness to respond and the quality of their responses? (Sometimes, reluctant responders gain confidence when they have increased thinking time and time to formulate responses with a partner.)

❏ After students are familiar with Think-Pair-Share, have students use it when they're holding discussions in small groups, and observe what happens. Do you see any change in the quality or quantity of their discussions?

Sharing and Reflection

❏ Try Think-Pair-Share in three different settings, such as a discussion of literature, a math problem-solving session, and a hands-on science activity. Do you notice any differences? Have a colleague do the same; compare notes and discuss your conclusions.

❏ Demonstrate Think-Pair-Share to your colleagues and have them discuss how they like it using it in their own discussions. Encourage them to try it in their classrooms, then get together again to compare notes.

APPENDIX

Teaching for Intelligence: Parameters for Change
by Eric J. Cooper and Daniel U. Levine

In the United States, emphasis on education reform for supporting social change has reached new heights through calls for change in the popular press, in educational journals, newsletters, and on the Internet. Yet, significant factors that will stall change reside in how reform is implemented, that is, the standards for what students know and need to know, how we implement professional development activities, and the ability of reformers to bridge the gap between policy and good implementation (Levine and Cooper 1991).

In many localities, school leaders call for teaching the Basics—often directing the district to curriculum that defines learning as separate discrete pieces of information with skills and knowledge taught independent of meaningful context (Berryman and Bailey 1992). Recent analyses point up the importance of teaching advanced thinking in the context of the subject matter and in conjunction with a new reality of the workplace. There can no longer be a dual track curriculum, one for a future engineer and another for an auto-trade journeyman (Barth 1997). Advanced thinking skills are *the* requisite for every student.

How localities deal with implementing change and the change process often determines the ability of a school system and community to remain competitive and viable in the global economy (White 1997). Initiating effective projects for improving thinking skills is an imposing challenge not to be taken lightly. Projects designed to improve thinking skills requires the following from an institutional structure:

- Creation of system-wide relatively large and complex programs to institute innovations.
- Adaptation of selected instructional materials to meet the demands of particular classrooms.
- Identification of core elements of the project that require strict adherence to maintain the integrity of the program—remaining elements can be modified at the classroom level.

Adapted from *Teaching for Intelligence I: A Collection of Articles*, edited by Barbara Z. Presseisen. ©1999 SkyLight Training and Publishing, Inc. Reprinted with permission of Eric J. Cooper and Daniel U. Levine and SkyLight Professional Development.

- Recognition of predictable obstacles such as traditional static thinking about maintaining discipline instead of achieving real learning outcomes.
- Use of authentic assessment approaches.

Perhaps second only to how a project is implemented, is the extent to which initiative and decision-making should promote "top-down" mandates or "bottom-up" participation. Top-down (administration at the district level to the classroom teacher) approaches tend to emphasize fidelity to a mandate as compared to a bottom-up model (classroom teacher to school or district) whose emphasis is on adaptation to the prevailing conditions in a particular classroom. Early on in the dialogue, many researchers and academic observers championed the need for teacher participation in initiating and guiding innovation. Recent research and analysis, however, seem to favor appropriately defined top-down initiatives.

Probably the best example of recent recognition of the role and possibilities of top-down leadership in bringing about successful change has been provided in longitudinal studies conducted by Miles (1983) and his colleagues. Miles summarized much of this research in an article in which he outlined the forces leading to "institutionalization" of innovation as follows:

> . . . high administrative commitment tends to lead to both administrative pressure on users to implement the innovation, along with administrative support, which often shows up in the form of assistance to users. Both the pressure and the assistance tend to lead to increased user effort. . . . the harder people worked at an innovation, the more committed they grew; that commitment was also fueled by increasing technical mastery of the innovation.
>
> Commitment and mastery both lead toward increasing stabilization of use . . . [which is] aided if administrators decide to mandate the innovation, which also naturally increases the percentage of use . . . [that in turn decisively encourages institutionalization]
>
> (Miles 1983, 18)

Emphasizing top-down action in bringing about change is not necessarily the same, of course, as de-emphasizing bottom-up participation. For one thing, the conclusions just quoted were concerned with institutionalization, not just initial mastery and implementation, and certainly Miles and his colleagues would be among the last researchers anywhere to ignore or play down the importance of teacher participation and commitment in designing and implementing innovation. In addition, their conclusions continue to emphasize the importance of "teacher-administrator harmony" and of "both teacher mastery/commitment and administrative action" (Miles 1983, 19). Nevertheless, their data and conclusions do provide an important balance to the work of some others who have tended to minimize the necessity for and possibilities of strong top-down mandates and action in carrying out innovation successfully.

Hall and Hord (1987) and Crandall, Eiseman, and Louis (1986) also have reviewed research related to the top-down/bottom-up issue and reached conclusions similar to those of Miles and his colleagues. Elaborating on some of the important considerations involved in devising and implementing innovations, Hall and Hord stressed that "mandates and decrees" are helpful in providing clear indications of priority, and Crandall, Eiseman, and Louis concluded that a strategy based on mandates by strong leaders "appears to require five elements: absence of debilitating conflict; an effective, debugged innovation; continuity of leadership; frequent reminders that successful and faithful implementation is important; and adequate resources and support" (Crandall, Eiseman, and Louis 1986, 40–41).

Implications from Research
The legacy of research from the 1980s is the conclusion that teachers must change their teaching practices in the direction of concentrating more time and effort on concept development, cognitive development, reasoning, thinking, higher-order comprehension skills, and advanced subject matter (Harris and Cooper 1985). A strong base of research linking cognitive development to prior knowledge in learning emerged in the late 1970s (Langer 1982). Those studies concluded that, particularly when reading is the learning mode, students with much prior knowledge and experience relevant to a subject have less difficulty learning new material and retain more than students with inadequate or incomplete prior knowledge and experience. Students need the benefit of teachers who know how to access prior knowledge that the students might not be aware of and that might help them with the material to be learned (Cooper and Sherk 1989).

Finding ways to help students relate what they already know to what is to be learned is often called preteaching or preparation.

Research has suggested that teachers accomplish this in several ways. One way is by encouraging students to make predictions before a reading and/or learning task (Cooper and Sherk 1989). Predicting, based on the students' prior knowledge of the topic of a reading selection and on what students think the reading selection will be about, helps students to become aware of their knowledge base. It also helps them to focus closely upon how the text informs the reader (Cooper and Sherk 1989).

Another transportable practice is to allow students to examine the structure of textual material before detailed reading takes place. For example, if students can determine that they are going to read a narrative selection, then they can review their knowledge of the narrative structure (i.e., a narrative has a setting, characters, plot beginning, and is often structured in terms of organizational patterns in time/sequence and problem/solution). If the selection is an expository one, students can be alerted to look for signals that indicate a particular relationship of ideas (organizational patterns such as cause-effect, comparison-contrast, and/or problem-solution; and chronology or sequence). Teachers are in the best position to point out such distinctions to their students and to determine how best to utilize the text for problem solving and decision making (Cooper and Sherk 1989).

In considering the ideas generally introduced in this brief article, readers should keep in mind the likelihood that innovations to improve instruction and change in thinking and other higher-order skills (e.g., reflective, critical, and creative analysis in the translation and application of knowledge) generally have to be relatively large and complex. Given the urgency in responding on a wider scale to deepening gulfs between American haves and have-nots, we cannot expect significant change to happen school by school, teacher by teacher. Many students are school-dependent for learning advanced skills—yet teachers have not had the support to be prepared in the past to offer other effective instruction to enhance higher-order skills (e.g., MacGinitie and MacGinitie 1986); the knowledge base for teaching thinking is still relatively small and undeveloped in terms of classroom practices (Marzano et al. 1987); emphasizing higher-order skills constitutes a major change in many or most classrooms and schools (Goodlad 1984; Perkins 1995); and many students need close guidance and assistance (i.e., mediation) from highly skilled teachers (Marzano et al. 1987).

The general complexity and large magnitude of change involved in innovative projects to improve instruction in thinking was underlined in an analysis of teaching thinking skills prepared by Nickerson, Perkins, and Smith (1985). Although the authors first pointed out that thinking-skills approaches vary considerably with respect to considerations such as the amount of class time devoted to instruction, the specific skills addressed, and the amount of special training for teachers, they also emphasized the general conclusions that teachers of thinking need to be facilitators of knowledge, that students must explore and discover knowledge rather than passively absorb it, that many teachers resist approaches that do not yet offer a clear and definite technology, that assessment of thinking skills is still relatively primitive, and that significant time-on-task opportunity has to be available to students. They further concluded that implementation of any thinking-skills programs should make sure that tasks generally are intrinsically interesting to students, that objectives and exercises should be "calibrated" to "students' current level of knowledge and abilities," that reasons for students' success or failure should be explicitly addressed, that considerable feedback should be provided for students, and that practice should be provided in "a variety of problem contexts" (Nickerson, Perkins, and Smith 1985, 342–343)—no small job for any classroom teacher. If we are to recognize the importance of teaching advanced thinking for preparing students to go to institutions of higher education, to successfully compete in the workplace of the present and future, and to become lifelong learners, we will have to recognize that sustained and cohesive professional development is necessary to reach our goals. Nothing less than total commitment by all stakeholders in school communities, state departments of education, and the federal government to this end will work.

References

Barth, P. (1997, November 26). Want to keep American jobs and avert class division? Try high school trip (A little physics goes a long way, too). *Education Week*, pp. 30-33.

Berryman, S. E., and T. R. Bailey. (1992). The double helix of education and the economy. New York: Teachers College Press.

Cooper, E. J., and J. Sherk. (1989). Addressing urban school reform: Issues and alliances. *Journal of Negro Education 58*, 3: 315-331.

Crandall, D. P., J. W. Eiseman, and K. S. Louis. (1986). Strategic planning issues that bear on the success of school improvement efforts. *Educational Administration Quarterly 22*, 3: 21–53.

Goodlad, J. I. (1984). A place called school. New York: McGraw-Hill.

Hall, G. E., and S. M. Hord. (1987). Change in schools. Albany: State University of New York Press.

Harris, T. L., and E. J. Cooper (1985). Reading, thinking, and concept development. New York: The College Board.

Langer, J. A. (1982). Facilitating text processing: The elaboration of prior knowledge. In J. A. Langer and M. Smith-Burke (Eds.), Reader meets author/Bridging the gap. Newark, DE: International Reading Association.

Levine, D. U., and E. J. Cooper. (1991). The change process and its implications in teaching thinking. In L. Idol and B. Jones (Eds.), Educational values and cognitive instruction: Implications for reform. Hillsdale, NJ: Lawrence Erlbaum Associates.

MacGinitie, W. H., and R. K. MacGinitie. (1986). Teaching students not to read. In S. DeCastell, A. Luke, and K. Egan (Eds.), Literacy, society, and schooling. Cambridge, England: Cambridge University Press.

Marzano, R. J., R. S. Brandt, C. S. Hughes, B. F. Jones, B. Z. Presseisen, S. C. Rankin, and C. Suhor. (1987). Dimensions of thinking. A framework for curriculum and instruction. Alexandria, VA: Association for Supervision and Curriculum Development.

Miles, M. B. (1983). Unraveling the mysteries of institutionalization. *Educational Leadership 41*, 2: 14-19.

Nickerson, R. S., D. N. Perkins, and E. E. Smith. (1985). The teaching of thinking. Hillsdale, NJ: Lawrence Erlbaum Associates.

Perkins, D. (1995). Outsmarting IQ—The emerging science of learnable intelligence. New York: Simon and Schuster.

White, K. A. (1997, November 26). Jobs will follow better schools, Miami-Dade leaders say. *Education Week*, p. 7.

BIBLIOGRAPHY

Beagle, P. S. 1991. *The last unicorn.* New York: Penguin.

Brett, J. 1996. *The mitten.* New York: Putnam.

Britton, J. 1970. *Language and learning.* London: Penguin.

Brooks, J. G., and M. G. Brooks. 1993. *The case for constructivist classrooms.* Alexandria, VA: Association for Supervision and Curriculum Development.

Carr, E., and D. Ogle. 1987. KWL plus: A strategy. *Journal of Reading* 30 (7): 626–631.

Cook, D. M., ed. 1989. *Strategic learning in the content areas.* Madison: Wisconsin Department of Public Instruction.

Dewey, J. 1916. *Democracy and education.* New York: Macmillan.

Dewey, J. 1963. *Experience and education.* New York: Collier.

Dixon, C., and D. Nessel. 1992. *Meaning making: Directed reading and thinking activities for second language students.* Englewood Cliffs, NJ: Alemany Press/Prentice Hall.

Duffy, G. C., and L. R. Roehler, eds. 1993. *Improving classroom reading instruction: A decision-making approach.* New York: Random House.

Elbow, P. 1975. *Writing without teachers.* 2d ed. New York: McGraw-Hill.

Farrell, C., and D. Nessel. 1984. *Word weaving: A teaching sourcebook for storytelling.* San Francisco: Zellerbach Family Fund.

Feuerstein, R. 1977. Mediated learning experience: A theoretical basis for cognitive human modifiability during adolescence. In P. Mitter (ed.), *Research to practice in mental retardation. Vol. II.* Baltimore: University Park Press.

———. 1978. The ontogeny of learning. In M. Brazier (ed.), *Brain mechanisms in memory and learning.* New York: Raven Press.

Grimm, J. 1998. *The Bremen town musicians.* New York: North-South Books.

Harris, T. L., and E. J. Cooper. 1985. *Reading, thinking, and concept development: Strategies for the classroom.* New York: The College Board.

Heimlich, J. E. and S. D. Puttelman. 1986. *Semantic mapping: Classroom applications.* Newark, DE: International Reading Association.

Herber, H. L. 1978. *Teaching reading in content areas.* 2d ed. Englewood Cliffs, NJ: Prentice-Hall.

Hyerle, D. 1996. *Visual tools for constructing knowledge.* Alexandria, VA: Association for Supervision and Curriculum Development.

Jones, B. F. 1988. SPaRCS in *Strategies for teaching reading as thinking: A teleconference resource guide.* Elmhurst, IL: North Central Regional Educational Laboratory.

Jones, B. F., A. S. Palincsar, D. S. Ogle, and E. G. Carr, eds. 1987. *Strategic teaching and learning: Cognitive instruction in the content areas.* Alexandria, VA: Association for Supervision and Curriculum Development.

Lewis, M., and D. Wray. 1995. *Developing student's non-fiction writing.* Warwickshire, England: Scholastic Ltd.

MacRorie, K. 1976. *Searching writing.* Rochelle Park, NJ: Hayden.

———. 1988. *The I search paper.* Portsmith, NH: Heinemann.

Martin, B. 1992. *Brown bear, brown bear, What do you see?* New York: Holt, Henry & Co.

Moffett, J. 1968. *A student-centered language arts curriculum K–13.* Boston: Houghton Mifflin.

Moore, D. W., J. E. Readence, and R. J. Rickelman. 1988. *Prereading activities for content area reading and learning.* Newark, DE: International Reading Association.

Nessel, D. 1985. Storytelling in the reading program. *The Reading Teacher* 38 (4): 378–381.

———. 1987. Reading comprehension: Asking the right questions. *Phi Delta Kappan* 68 (6): 442–444.

———.1988. Channeling knowledge for reading expository text. *Journal of Reading* 32 (3): 231–235.

Nessel, D., M. Jones, and C. Dixon. 1989. *Thinking through the language arts.* New York: Macmillan.

Nichols, J. 1980. Using paragraph frames to help remedial high school students with written assignments. *Journal of Reading* 24 (3): 228–231.

Ogle, D. M. 1986. K-W-L: A teaching model that develops active reading of expository text. *The Reading Teacher* 40 (5): 564–570.

Sendak, P. 1985. *Grandpa's house*. S. Barofsky, trans. New York: HarperCollins.

Shah, I. 1979. *World tales*. New York: Harcourt.

Smith, P., and G. Tompkins. 1988. Structured notetaking: A new strategy for content area readers. *Journal of Reading* 32 (1): 46–53.

Stevenson, P. 1999. *Hansel and Gretel*. New York: Scholastic.

Tolkien, J. R. R. 1966. *The hobbit*. New York: Houghton Mifflin.

Torbe, M. and P. Medway. 1982. *The climate for learning*. Montclair, NJ: Boynton/Cook.

Vacca, R. T., and J. L. Vacca. 1989. *Content area reading*. 3d ed. Reading, MA: Addison-Wesley.

Vygotsky, L. 1978. *Mind in society*. Cambridge, MA: Harvard University Press.

Weaver, C. 1994. *Reading process and practice: From sociopsycholinguistics to whole language*. 2d ed. Portsmouth, NH: Heinemann.

Withrow, J., G. Brookes, and M. C. Cummings. 1990. *Changes: Readings for ESL writers*. New York: St. Martin's Press.

INDEX

Advanced thinking skills, 90
The Algonquin Cinderella (Shah), 74
Analogies, 2–5
Anticipation guide, 6–9
Authentic assessment, 91
Authentic discourse, xi–xii

Basics, teaching the, 90
Brown Bear, Brown Bear, What Do You See? (Martin), 30

Causal relationship, graphic organizers for, 20
Cause-effect patterns, 93
  and frame paragraphs, 15
Character journals, 33–34, 37
Chronological order patterns, and frame paragraphs, 15
Chronology patterns, 93
Classroom interactions, effective, viii
Comparison/contrasting patterns, x–xi, 93
  and frame paragraphs, 15
Comprehension skills, strip stories in building, 77
Constructing meaning, xi
Creative thinking, ix
Critical thinking, ix, xi
Cubing, 10–13, 18

Detecting relationships, xi
Dialogue, writing, for Readers' Theater, 63
Discussing in storytelling, 74
Double-entry journals, 33, 34–35
Double-entry notes, 51

Dramatizing in storytelling, 74
Drawing in storytelling, 74

Education reform, 90
Evaluating, xi
Expository writing
  I-Search Reports as, 24
  keywords for, 38–39
Eye-witness report, saturation reporting as, 69

Factual statements with anticipation guides, 9
Focused freewriting, 18, 19
  and cubing, 10, 11–12
Frame paragraph, 14–16
Freewriting, 17–19
  focused, 18, 19
  and cubing, 10, 11–12
  student guidelines for unfocused, 18

Graphic organizers, 20–23
  T-chart, 22
  Venn diagram, 21
Graphics, notes as, 51

Hansel and Gretel (Stevenson), 74
Higher-order thinking skills, 93

Imitation writing, 28–31
In Grandpa's House (Sendak), 30
Institutionalization of innovation, 91–92
Intelligence, teaching for, 90–94
Introduction, anticipation guides in, 8
I-Search Report, 24–27

Journals, 32–37
    character, 33–34, 37
    double-entry, 33, 34–35
    Reader Response, 33, 36

Keywords, 38–41
KWHL, 44
KWL, 42–45

Language arts
    anticipation guides in, 8
    I-Search Reports in, 24
    saturation reporting in, 69
The Last Unicorn (Beagle), 30
Learning logs, 33, 36–37, 37
List-Group-Label, 46–49
Literature
    Possible Sentences to introduce, 56
    Think-Pair-Share in, 87

Main idea/detail notes, 51
Math
    double-entry journals for, 35
    Think-Pair-Share in, 87
The Mitten (Brett), 74

National Urban Alliance for Effective Education (NUA), vii–viii
Notes
    double-entry, 51
    as graphics, 51
    main idea/detail, 51
    taking, 50–53

Observing, x–xi

Paragraph, frame, 14–16
Possible Sentences, 54–57
Predictions, 92–93
Prereading activity
    List-Group-Label strategy as, 46
    Possible Sentences as, 54
    strip stories as, 80

PQRST (Preview, Question, Read, Summarize, Test), 67
Prewriting
    cubing as, 10
    freewriting as, 17
    List-Group-Label strategy as, 46
    Think-Pair-Share as, 86
Prior knowledge, 92
    graphic organizers in activating, 20
    KWL in activating, 42
    List-Group-Label strategy in activating, 46
Probing questions and keywords, 39
Problem-solution patterns, 93

Question wall, 27

Reader Response Journals, 33, 36
Readers' Theater, 62–65
Read-Talk-Write, 58–61
Reflection, vii
Report, I-Search, 24–27
Reporting, saturation, 69–72
Research, legacy of, 92–93
Restating/paraphrasing, 66–68

Saturation reporting, 69–72
Science
    analogies in, 4
    double-entry journals for, 35
    keywords to introducing topics in, 40, 41
    notetaking in, 52
    Possible Sentences to introduce materials, 56
    Think-Pair-Share in, 87
Sentences, possible, 54–57
Sequence patterns, 93
Social studies
    analogies in, 4
    imitation writing for, 30–31
    keywords to introducing topics in, 40, 41

Social studies (continued)
    note taking in, 52
    Possible Sentences to introduce, 56
    Readers' Theater for, 64
    saturation reports in, 71
Statements of opinion with anticipation guides, 9
Story, strip, 77–81
Story Notebook, 76
Storytelling, 73–76
Strip story, 77–81
SQ3R (Survey, Question, Read, Recite, Review), 67
Syntactical pattern, 29

T-chart, 22
Team webbing, 82–84
Textual material, examining structure of, 93

Thinking
    modes of, ix
    purposes for, x
    skills in, x
Think-Pair-Share, 85–87
Top-down approaches, 91

Venn diagram, 21

Webbing, team, 82–84
Wrap-up questions with anticipation guides, 8
Writing. *See also* Expository writing
    dialogue, 63
    imitation, 28–31
    in storytelling, 74

There are
one-story intellects,
two-story intellects, and three-story
intellects with skylights. All fact collectors, who
have no aim beyond their facts, are one-story minds. Two-story minds
compare, reason, generalize, using the labors of the fact collectors
as well as their own. Three-story minds idealize, imagine,
predict—their best illumination comes from
above, through the skylight.
—*Oliver Wendell*
Holmes

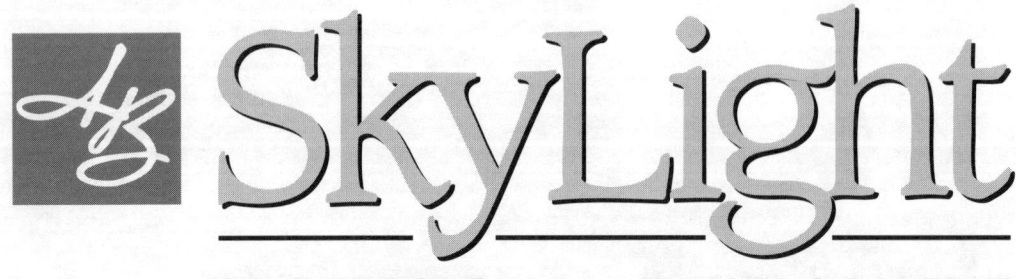

SkyLight
PROFESSIONAL DEVELOPMENT

We Prepare Your Teachers Today for the Classrooms of Tomorrow

Learn from Our Books and from Our Authors!

Ignite Learning in Your School or District.

SkyLight's team of classroom-experienced consultants can help you foster systemic change for increased student achievement.

Professional development is a process not an event. SkyLight's experienced practitioners drive the creation of our on-site professional development programs, graduate courses, research-based publications, interactive video courses, teacher-friendly training materials, and online resources—call SkyLight Professional Development today.

SkyLight specializes in three professional development areas.

Specialty # 1 — Best Practices
We **model** the best practices that result in improved student performance and guided applications.

Specialty # 2 — Making the Innovations Last
We help set up **support** systems that make innovations part of everyday practice in the long-term systemic improvement of your school or district.

Specialty # 3 — How to Assess the Results
We prepare your school leaders to encourage and **assess** teacher growth, **measure** student achievement, and **evaluate** program success.

Contact the SkyLight team and begin a process toward long-term results.

SkyLight Professional Development
2626 S. Clearbrook Dr., Arlington Heights, IL 60005
800-348-4474 • 847-290-6600 • FAX 847-290-6609
info@skylightedu.com • www.skylightedu.com